JOB RELATIONS

10-Hour Sessions Outline
and
Reference Material

JOB RELATIONS

A TRAINING WITHIN INDUSTRY PROGRAM

The Training Within Industry program of Job Relations was developed in order to provide management with a tool whereby supervisors could acquire the skill of leadership.

The material in the "Job Relations Sessions Outlines" covers the content as handled in five 2-hour meetings for a group of ten supervisors.

CRC Press
Taylor & Francis Group
Boca Raton London New York

CRC Press is an imprint of the
Taylor & Francis Group, an **informa** business

Originally published as *Job Relations: 10-Hour Sessions Outline and Reference Material*, released in 1944 by the War Manpower Commission of the Bureau of Training, Washington, District of Columbia.

First published 2009 by Enna Products Corporation.

Published 2023 by CRC Press
Taylor & Francis Group
6000 Broken Sound Parkway NW, Suite 300
Boca Raton, FL 33487-2742

2009 edition ©Taylor & Francis Group, LLC
CRC Press is an imprint of Taylor & Francis Group, an Informa business

No claim to original U.S. Government works

ISBN-13: 978-1-897363-94-2 (pbk)

Visit the Taylor & Francis Web site at
http://www.taylorandfrancis.com

and the CRC Press Web site at
http://www.crcpress.com

Distributed by Productivity Press

Cover Design/Illustrations by Khemanand Shiwram
Editor: Collin McLoughlin
Associate Editor: Shawna Gilleland

Library of Congress Control Number: 2009938938

Library of Congress Cataloging-in-Publication Data

United States. Bureau of Training. War Manpower Commission. 1944
        Job Relations: 10-Hour Sessions Outline and Reference Material
            1. Training Within Industry   2. Training of employees 3. Organizational change
    4. Productivity–Increasing through training   I. Title

Dedicated to the men and women of The Greatest Generation.

WAR MANPOWER COMMISSION

WASHINGTON, D.C.

July 1944.

To The War Production Trainer:

Your Job Relations sessions can have for your plant and for the war production effort a constructive influence, perhaps never before experienced. You have an unusual <u>opportunity</u> of influencing supervisors to improve their everyday relationships on the job.

Giving workers technical skill alone is not enough. Supervisors must give every man and woman at work the leadership that enlists cooperation and teamwork. You can help supervisors to get this skill of working with people—it is your <u>obligation</u> to stress its importance to them.

You should strive with all the energy and diligence you possess to lead each Job Relations group in the very best way possible—and to do a <u>better</u> job with each succeeding group.

To ensure a uniformly high standard, work from this outline <u>always</u>. Do not deviate from it. Do not trust to your memory, regardless of the number of sessions you put on.

Once again, leadership in Job Relations presents an <u>opportunity</u> and an <u>obligation</u>.

Sincerely,

C. R. Dooley

C. R. Dooley, Director,

Training Within Industry Service.

SUMMARY OF PURPOSE AND EMPHASIS OF JOB RELATIONS SESSIONS

I To establish the fact that everyday job relationships are one of the most important parts of the war production supervisor's job.
To present the foundations for good relations.
To establish a 4-step method for meeting job relations situations.

A supervisor gets results through people. People must be treated as individuals. Good supervision prevents many problems, but the supervisor must know how to handle those that do arise.

II To develop skill in Step 1, "Get the Facts."
To give the group practice on Step 1 through emphasis on this step in a problem presented by the Trainer, and to give members of the group practice in looking at the 4-step method in two problems brought in by supervisors.

Complete facts must be known or obtained. Opinions and feelings must be found out and considered along with facts. It is necessary to look at an individual because all people are not alike.

III To develop skill in Step 2, "Weigh and Decide."
To give the group practice on Step 2 through emphasis on this step in a problem presented by the Trainer and to give members of the group practice in three problems brought in by supervisors.

Decisions are made on the basis of facts properly evaluated and related.

IV To establish the importance of Steps 3 and 4, "Take Action" and "Check Results."
To give the group practice in Steps 3 and 4 through emphasis on these steps in a problem presented by the Trainer and to give members of the group practice in looking at the 4-step method in three problems brought in by supervisors.

The supervisor must know his responsibility. He must watch the timing of his action and follow-up, and watch for effect on the objective, on the individual, on the group, and on production.

V To give members of the group practice in looking at the 4-step method in two problems brought in by supervisors.
To review and summarize foundations, 4-step method, and tips for getting opinions and feelings.
To consider the other working relationships of the supervisor—to other operating departments, to staff departments, and to his boss.

Further develop the habit of using the complete method. Point out application of the method to supervisor's other relationships. A supervisor gets results through people.

CONTENTS

Contents

Strategy for Job Relations

Training Within Industry looks at the training of supervisors as a five-part job. That is, the supervisor has five needs.

1.   Knowledge of the Work
2.   Knowledge of Responsibilities
3.   Skill in Instructing
4.   Skill in Improving Methods
5.   Skill in Leading

Job Relations is a streamlined, intensive program designed to give operating supervisors practice in developing Skill in Leading. It is not intended to provide any training in the "Knowledge of Responsibilities" area—the job of training supervisors in the policies, agreements, and regulations of a particular plant must be done by the plant—and it assumes that a supervisor has a Knowledge of the Work.

Job Relations aims to develop a skill—not to give stock answers to personnel questions or problems, or to provide industrial relations background on such subjects as rates of pay, safety, etc.

Since Job Relations is focused on working with people, descriptions of what happens to people are the materials for this program. In the standard Sessions Outlines there are four of these problems, each of which is used at the specific point for a particular reason. The time of the members of the group is spent mostly on the handling of their own problems which they bring in for group discussion.

Job Relations is limited to groups of ten supervisors. Experience has shown that this number is desirable. A smaller group does not provide enough variety of problems and a larger group provides too much material for inclusion within the ten hours.

In some instances observers have been admitted to the sessions with the purpose of giving them familiarity with the contents of the program as it normally operates. These observers are requested to stay in character as observers and are not permitted to join in the discussion. When there are observers present it should be made clear to them in advance that they are not being asked to attend in order to assist in lining up how the program should operate—this is a standardized program and no deviations or changes are to be made.

Training Within Industry urges the use of this program for all of the plant's first-line and second-line supervisors. Those who are new to the job of directing the work of other people need help and training more than those who have had experience on the job.

However, if management says that all its supervisors would benefit by this way of looking at employee relationships or that the pressure of present production conditions has brought about an increase in the problems which a supervisor must handle, the same training program will apply to persons who have been on higher level jobs for some time. The nature of the problems brought in and the discussion may be quite different from those in a group of new, first-line supervisors.

If in such a group, their problems tend to be unanimously well handled and the Trainer should make a specific appeal for the bringing in of situations which have had poor results, and also for the kind which may be sized up in advance to get good results through preventive action.

Out of the experience of preparing this program good reasons have developed for doing what is done, in the way it is done, and at a particular time.

SESSION I—PRESENTATION OF FOUNDATIONS FOR GOOD

RELATIONS AND THE 4-STEP METHOD

Getting Acquainted

Ask each man in the group about his own background and present supervisory job. This brings quick and easy participation from every member of the group. The members are being asked to tell something about which they and only they have the story. Also, the Trainer gains valuable information about the people with whom he will be working for the next ten hours.

The Supervisor's Five Needs

The five needs are discussed to emphasize to supervisors that, regardless of their industry or department, they must be well versed in two knowledges and three skills in order to be effective supervisors. One of these needs is the Skill of Leading, which is covered in these sessions.

Chart on Supervisory Responsibility

The development of the chart with "people" in the center and the arrow linking the supervisor to the people is a quick means of focusing attention on the subject-matter of Job Relations. There is also real group participation in the development of this chart, as members point out their responsibilities.

Foundations for Good Relations

There are certain basic points which are followed by effective supervisors. While Job Relations does not give a great deal of time in the ten hours to these foundations as such, nevertheless it is necessary to recognize their importance and to put them across in a way which will gain acceptance. They form the underlying spirit of good relationships and promote good supervision.

Chart on the Individual

The pulling out of one person from the group of people through whom the supervisor gets results is done because of the need of pointing out that people must be treated as individuals since they are different in background, interests, and tastes.

The Joe Smith Problem

This problem is told by the Trainer. It is short and the telling gives it much more reality than reading. Also, the members of the group will be telling their problems later, and the Trainer should set the pattern he wishes used.

This situation was handled in a way that got poor results. Such a problem was chosen for several reasons. First, it will often be necessary for the group to be critical about the results which a supervisor gets when he does not use the complete 4-step method. It is easier to start this pattern presenting a problem which does not personally concern any member of the group.

Second, the problem is a very simple one from which it is easy to pull out the positive points which need to be made. Asking where the supervisor skidded almost invariably sets up the main points of Job Relations' 4-step method.

The telling of the problem is broken into two parts in order to get emphasis for the importance of starting the 4-step pattern at the beginning—getting facts before attempting to make a decision and take action. The discussion begins in the pattern which will be followed throughout. That is, it is necessary to first pull out just what the supervisor is trying to accomplish. This pattern of discussion enables the leader to keep away from the criticism of decisions by focusing on the use of the method. The four main steps on the card are pulled out from the Joe Smith problem. Experience has shown that the discussion is belabored if the attempt is made to also develop the sub-points.

How Problems Arise

This material is presented in order to show supervisors that they often can get in on situations early; that an advance size-up may prevent problems. This also will suggest to members of the group other problems which they might bring into the discussion.

Problem Sheets

The problem sheets are used to get conviction from the group that the Job Relations program is aimed at the kinds of problems that supervisors encounter every day. It also gives hints on the type of problems which the members of the group will bring in for discussion.

Requests for Problems

Members of the group prefer to talk about their own problems rather than those brought in by the Trainer. The four standard problems are used because it is necessary to insure that certain points of the method are put across. But, once these points are worked in, the rest of the time is given to the problems which the men themselves are living with every day. The problems are restricted to those which are within the supervisor's own job to handle, something he can and must do something about.

SESSION II—IMPORTANCE OF GETTING THE FACTS

The Tom Problem

This problem is chosen to show the necessity of getting the facts and the importance of remembering that opinions and feelings must be considered the same as facts. The problem also gives some hints as to the way in which you get personal facts.

This problem is read, as exact words are important. Since it must be well read, which involves previous practice, it is specified that the Trainer read both parts of the dialogue.

This particular problem points to the difference between facts about the man and facts about the machine—both are necessary in order to have the whole story. The members of the group are also given a hint that it is sometimes necessary to probe a bit for the meaning behind words.

This problem points out the special importance of handling confidential material properly.

At a number of places the Trainer stops reading in order that the group may discuss specific points. It is possible in this way to get recognition of a few of the tips for getting personal opinions and feelings, which will later be developed and summarized.

Problems Brought in by Supervisors

In the first supervisor's problem, and all succeeding ones, the man who is to present a problem should come to the head of the table with the Trainer. It has been found that shifting of position in the room is welcome and there appears to be a certain advantage in focusing on the man in this particular way. In the handling of the supervisor's problem the objective is pulled out to open the discussion. The Trainer must at all times be careful to key the comments, to "Did he follow the 4 steps?"—not to "Did he make a good decision?" The discussion must be handled so that the supervisor who presents the problem gets practice in using the 4 steps (see Standard Procedure, Reference Section).

Request to Consider Several Problems

Since occasionally a group member who is new or reluctant to talk does not wish to bring a problem for discussion, and also because some problems are so simple that any lengthy discussion would be belabored, it is sometimes necessary to have more than one problem from some members.

If a man says that he does not have any problems in his department, review the problem sheet again and ask such questions as "Does output ever fall off?" "Did anyone ever ask for a raise?" "Are any changes coming?" etc. If the man is obviously unwilling to present a problem after spending some time on reconsidering kinds of problems, do not press him too far. This would be poor Job Relations. (He cannot, however, be certified if he does not present a problem.) Personal coaching may help a man who is reluctant to present a problem.

Request for Problems with Poor Results

If all problems are well handled, discussion is not as interesting as if a diagnostic technique can be used to show where the supervisor skidded.

SESSION III—BASIS FOR DECISIONS

The session is opened by showing that a doctor, in getting the symptoms of a patient, goes through a process quite like the Job Relations 4-step method. Comparison with the doctor is used to show that the 4-step method has universal application, that it is specifically followed in a prominent profession, and perhaps, most important of all, to show that the doctor needs and gets much confidential information which he must handle well or it will not again be available to him.

The Shipyard Problem

This situation, which ended in poor results, is used to stress Step 2, "Weigh and Decide." It brings out the necessity of using all the facts and weighing them before making a final decision. The poor decision was reached because the supervisor first did not properly evaluate the facts which he had, and second, because he did not have the whole story.

SESSION IV—CHECKING RESULTS OF PREVENTIVE ACTION

The problem of the first Woman Supervisor is used as an example of good results of preventive action. The problem involves a number of people, and the subject is one which is current in many war production plants. The members of the group are also given a tip to work through those people who are recognized as natural, but informal, leaders.

Effect of Change

This subject is brought up to show that the problem of the first Woman Supervisor is not a "Woman" problem, but one typifying "change." Change is usually resented, and supervisors need to take preventive action.

SESSION V—A SUPERVISOR'S OTHER WORK RELATIONSHIPS

Request for Statements on Use of Job Relations

By getting the members themselves to pull out the advantages to them, personally, of following a method which will improve the quality of decisions and actions and which also shows the importance of checking results, the selling of Job Relations is completed.

Chart

The supervisor's responsibility chart, as used in Session I, is now amplified in order to point out to the supervisor the important position which he is in and to give recognition to it. This chart also offers the opportunity of again stressing "Get the Facts." The Trainer develops the idea that getting the facts will be useful in any relationship that the supervisor has, and that in a number of cases he will be responsible for giving the facts.

Closing Statement

The members of the group must leave with the feeling that what they do does matter, that it is very important. When the Trainer has made this point the session should be ended no matter what time it is. After a high point has once been reached, the whole effect can be ruined by keeping the members straining at a discussion in order to fill the hours.

INTRODUCTION OF JOB RELATIONS TRAINER BY MANAGEMENT REPRESENTATIVE

(Trainer to provide Management representative with copy of this page)

Job Relations is:

> a streamlined program for war industry from Training Within Industry
>
> drawn from experienced supervisors in industry.

The management:

> has approved this program
>
> wants it for this plant
>
> expects you to attend each session, and be here on time.

This is *your* meeting —

> no reports are going to be made to management, except on attendance.

There will be:

> 5 two-hour meetings
>
> held at _____ in _____ room, on _____

This program is important:

> management expects you to do a good job—includes good relations with the people you supervise
>
> management knows you are going to get some real help
>
> this method will show you how to be a more effective supervisor.

This is Mr. _____

JOB RELATIONS TRAINER'S INTRODUCTION WHEN NO MANAGEMENT REPRESENTATIVE ATTENDS

I am _____

Management:

    has approved the Job Relations Program

    wants it for this plant.

Job Relations is:

    a streamlined program for war industry from Training Within Industry

    drawn from experienced supervisors in industry.

This is *our* meeting —

    no reports will be made to management, except on attendance.

There will be:

    5 two-hour meetings

    held at _____ in _____ room, on _____

CODE

CAPITALS . . . . Section Heads

Horizontal line across page . . . . Encloses section for timing

Plain type . . . . Trainer says in own words

★ Star in front of line . . . . Trainer says verbatim

Material between lines . . . . Board Work

Bracket . . . . Instruction to trainer

PRESENTATION OF FOUNDATIONS FOR GOOD RELATIONS AND 4-STEP METHOD

Time
Table
Allow
5 min

INTRODUCTION BY MANAGEMENT

(recommended procedure)

> Give management representative copy of outline (page xviii). Best results are obtained when a management representative opens the session.

> Introduction by trainer (emergency only). Use outline (page xix) when impossible to get management representative to open the session.

5 min
to here

Allow
10 min

GETTING ACQUAINTED

> Tell something about your own background of supervisory experience. This is important even if you know all members of the group.

> Have supervisors introduce themselves.
> Use name cards.
>> Ask each man to tell you :
>> work—department—number supervised—supervisory experience.

> If there are observers, explain:
>> They wish to know more about the program.
>> They do not enter the discussion, ask questions, or make remarks.

> Stress:—our meeting—problems discussed here are confidential—no names—give reasons—get agreement.

15 min
to here

Those who attend all five sessions and present a problem will receive certificates.

Allow
10 min

DISCUSS THE SUPERVISOR'S FIVE NEEDS

In these meetings we are going to use the term "supervisor" a great deal.

★ For the purpose of our discussions when we refer to the
★ supervisor we mean anybody in charge of people, or
★ who directs the work of others.

We are all supervisors.

Good supervisors have always realized that they have five needs.

Let's take a look at these needs. They are:

★ 1. Knowledge of the Work

★ 2. Knowledge of Responsibilities

★ 3. Skill in Improving Methods

★ 4. Skill in Instructing

★ 5. Skill in Leading

> Count the five needs on your fingers as you enumerate.

1. *Knowledge of the Work* refers to the kind of information which makes your business different from all other businesses:

materials	tools	operations
machines	processes	technical skill

Many a person has spent his lifetime in his work and is still acquiring knowledge of it. If he moves to another industry, a new Knowledge of Work has to be learned.

We are not going to attempt to meet this need in these sessions.

2. *Knowledge of Responsibilities* refers to the particular company situation regarding:

policies	regulations	agreements
rules	safety rules	schedules
	interdepartmental relationships	

These are different in every company. Hence this Knowledge of Responsibilities must be supplied locally.

Every supervisor, to do his job, must have a clear understanding of his authority and responsibilities as a part of management.

These local responsibilities are the "ground rules" under which every supervisor has to work—but we are not going to attempt to meet this need in these sessions.

3. *Skill in Instructing* is concerned with helping supervisors develop a well-trained work force:

- have less scrap, re-work, and rejects
- have fewer accidents
- have less tool and equipment damage

This skill is practiced in Job Instruction sessions.

4. *Skill in Improving Methods* deals in utilizing materials, machines, and manpower more effectively by having supervisors study each operation in order to combine, rearrange, and simplify details of the job.

This skill is practiced in Job Methods sessions.

5. *Skill in Leading* helps the supervisor to improve his ability in working with people.

There are basic principles that, when applied day in and day out, will tend to keep relations smooth and prevent problems from arising.

By pointing out the ways that problems do arise one can readily see that preventive action can be taken.

This applies particularly in anticipating changes that may not be readily accepted and in sensing changes in output, attitudes, and relationships.

However, when problems do arise, there is an organized procedure to handle such problems that helps get better results from the action we take.

> STRESS THE FACT THAT SKILLS ARE ACQUIRED BY PRACTICE.

The supervisor is not born with this skill. He must acquire it by actual practice. Just as soon as this skill is acquired by a supervisor he becomes more effective in the doing of his job. In these five two-hour sessions, we will discuss this Skill in Leading, which we shall call Job Relations.

DESCRIBE SUPERVISOR'S PROBLEMS AS REGARDS JOB RELATIONS

1. Too few people realize that the supervisor's job is complex and difficult.

Management wants *output* and *quality*.

Output and quality always require the loyalty and cooperation of people in addition to what machines can accomplish.

Can we do something which will improve loyalty and cooperation? That is the purpose of these meetings.

When a machine is installed in a department, a handbook comes with it, or there may be a mechanic specially qualified in how that particular piece of machinery works, and directions on how to keep it in good operating condition, or what to do when it breaks down.

Supervisors get new people all the time, but handbooks don't come with them.

How are you going to keep those new persons in top form? What will you do if they fail?

Employees will tend to judge the whole plant in terms of the treatment they receive from their immediate boss.

Remember your first day on the job? I still remember mine. (Illustrate)

There are thousands of people in supervisory positions today who were operators a short time ago.

As time goes on, thousands more men and women will have to assume supervisory jobs.

Some of these people—some men, some women, have long backgrounds as operators, some do not.

These new supervisors *must* quickly learn to work *through* people.

They must recognize that they can get their jobs done only through the cooperation of the people whose work they direct.

Supervisors, new and old alike, are confronted with the problem of obtaining the cooperation of:

- people who have never worked before
- people who have had steady work but of a different nature

Newly appointed supervisors also may have the problem of obtaining the cooperation of people who:

- know more about the technical aspects of the job than they do
- have many more years of service than they have

Try to get agreement.

To meet such problems some kind of training in the special skill of leading is necessary.

This skill of working with people has long been recognized as a mark of good supervision.

2. What do we mean by "good supervision"?

★ Good supervision means that the supervisor gets the
★ people in his department to do what he wants done,
★ *when* it should be done, and the way he wants it done,
★ because *they* want to do it.

4

★ 3. Now, in these sessions I'm not going to tell you how
★ to run your job.

But experienced supervisors have developed a skill in working with people.

This skill can be learned.

It saves supervisors a lot of headaches.

Let's see what we can find out about this skill.

SHOW THAT A SUPERVISOR MEETS HIS RESPONSIBILITIES THROUGH RELATIONSHIPS WITH PEOPLE

★ 1. What are the common titles for different levels of
★ supervision in this shop?

These may be suggested:

lead man	crew chief	group leader
gang boss	supervisor	foreman

★ For the purpose of our discussion, when we refer to a
★ "supervisor" we mean ANYBODY WHO IS IN CHARGE
★ OF PEOPLE OR WHO DIRECTS THE WORK OF OTHERS.

Write "Supervisor" and enclose in a box near top of left third of board.

Supervisor

I was in a group not long ago where one supervisor said, "I make wire." Did that supervisor himself make wire? No, he supervised a department in which many people worked together to turn out the wire.

Write *above* Supervisor:

A supervisor gets results through people

5

Let's look at what you do as a supervisor.

We will let this circle represent the supervisory job.

> Draw a circle under supervisor.

**A supervisor gets results
through people**

> **Supervisor**

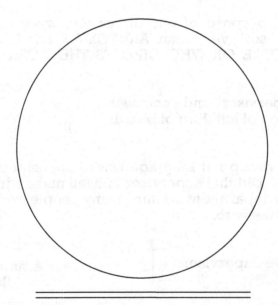

2. Let's look at the things for which your boss holds you responsible.

★ Of course, our boss
★ holds us responsible
★ for production.

Write Production in one segment.

★ Besides production,
★ for what else does
★ your boss hold you
★ responsible?

As members suggest kinds of supervisory responsibilities, write the name and outline the segment. Write down whatever is mentioned, but try to include those on the chart at right.

A supervisor gets results through people

Supervisor

Any of the following suggestions may be offered:

reports   plant protection
scrap   schedules
morale

Leave top section of the circle unlabeled.

★ We will let this section represent all other responsibilities
★ of the supervisor.

★ 3. We won't try to define the whole supervisory job —
★ instead let's see if there is anything in common about
★ these responsibilities.

Who gets out production?

> Do not spend too much time getting the answer, which is "People." Give it yourself if someone does not give this answer.

> Put small circles in the "Production" segment.

★ These represent
★ people.

Whom do you train?

> When someone says "People," put in other circles in segment marked "Training."

> Continue until there are small circles in every segment including the blank one.
>
> You can say:

How do you get quality?

Who gets hurt?

> Use "who" questions.

A supervisor gets results through people

Supervisor

8

Is there any part of the supervisor's job which does not involve people?

No.

Place circles in blank segment.

When we look at any part of the supervisor's job, we find people in the situation.

Enclose small circles in a hub.

Erase most of the small circles and write PEOPLE inside the hub.

The supervisor gets results through people.

Point to heading.

A supervisor gets results through people

Supervisor

★ In order to meet these
★ responsibilities there
★ must be some
★ relationship between
★ the supervisor and
★ each of his people.

★ Let's have this line rep-
★ resent that relationship.

Draw double-headed
arrow and label it
Job Relations.

Job Relations are the
everyday relations
between you and the
people you supervise.

The kind of relations
you have affects the
kind of results you get.

Relations with some
are good, with others
are poor, but there are
always relationships.

Poor relationships cause
poor results; good
relationships cause
good results.

Illustrate by use of chart.

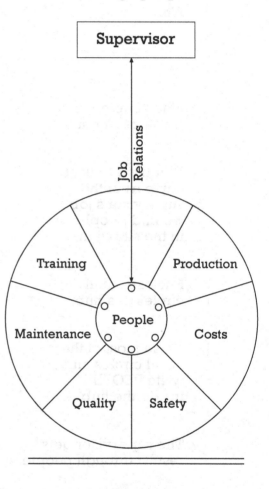

**A supervisor gets results
through people**

Supervisor

Job Relations

Training

Production

Maintenance

People

Costs

Quality

Safety

*45 min
to here*

When a supervisor wants to meet any of these responsibilities
effectively, he must have good relations with his people.

PRESENT FOUNDATIONS FOR GOOD RELATIONS

Experience shows that successful supervisors use definite foundations for good relations. *They find that these foundations keep the job relations line strong.*

| Write on top center of board the heading | **Foundations for Good Relations** |

★ 1. There are some things that you and I as supervisors
★ can do, day in and day out, about keeping the job
★ relations line in good condition.
★ For instance, we can let each worker know how he is
★ getting along.

| Write under heading: | **Let each worker know how he is getting along** |

Suppose a man goes home and someone says "How are you doing on your job?" and he has to say, "I don't know—no one's said anything."

Do you think that's good job relations if the man feels uncertain about important things like his job?

We know it isn't.

Do you think it is a good idea to let each worker know how he is getting along?

Wouldn't you like to know how you are getting along? I like to.

I wonder if these people [point to board] would like to know how they are getting along. Wouldn't that strengthen that job relations line?

★ 2. Another foundation for good job relations is
★ "Give credit when due."

| Write on board: | **Give credit when due** |

If a man has been sick but stays on at work to finish an important job, maybe you can't give him a raise, but you can let him know it helped you.

Do you think it is good job relations to give credit when due? Is that the kind of treatment you like?

I wonder if these people [point to board] wouldn't like it. Would it help the job relations line if we did give people credit when due?

★ 3. Another foundation for good relations is,
★ "Tell people in advance about changes
★ that will affect them."

| Write on board: | **Tell people in advance about changes that will affect them** |

Suppose someone tells you tonight that beginning tomorrow you're going to transfer to the midnight shift and start to work at midnight instead of at 8:00 in the morning?

Are you going to like it?

Are you going to think about your car pool?

You at least want a chance to have your say.

Would it be a good idea to tell people in advance about changes that affect them?

Do you think that would help the job relations line?

I wonder if these people [point to board] wouldn't like to know in advance about changes that affect them.

★ 4. Another foundation for good relations is,
★ "Make best use of each person's ability."

| Write on board: | **Make best use of each person's ability** |

Have you ever had a man who went sour just because he felt he could do more skilled work than you gave him to do?

Have you ever looked around your shop to see if you had that job for him?

Do you think it would help the job relations line if we made the best use of each person's ability?

I wonder if we are making the best use of the ability of these people [point to board].

These foundations are important to everyone. Using them will smooth job relations and assist us as supervisors to meet our responsibilities [point to board work].

12

The board will look like this:

A supervisor gets results through people

Foundations for Good Relations

Supervisor

Job Relations

Training

Production

People

Maintenance

Costs

Quality

Safety

Let each worker know how he is getting along.

Give credit when due.

Tell people in advance about changes that will affect them.

Make best use of each person's ability.

DEVELOP THE "INDIVIDUAL" CHART

Time Table Allow 10 min

★ Does this mean that all these people are alike? The
★ answer is no. People are different and must be treated
★ as individuals.

> Write on top right
> third of board:

People must be treated as individuals

All right, no two of us are alike.

Let's pull out one of these persons and see why he is different.

> Draw a dotted line extending from one of the small circles to
> another big circle. Label it AN INDIVIDUAL. Do not erase the
> foundations.

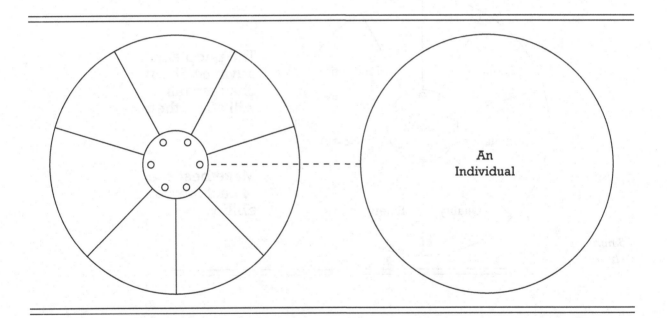

We'll let this circle represent any one of these people.

★ So let's take a look at this employee and what affects
★ him as an individual. We know that his job is a big factor.

14

Write His Job on left
one-third segment
of circle.

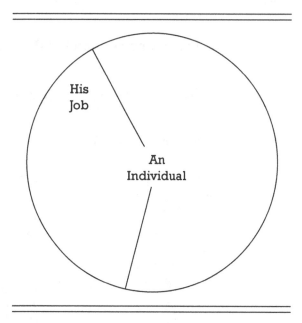

Now what else? What other things
affect him as an individual? What
makes one toolmaker different from
another toolmaker?

Write in interests as
members suggest.
Be sure to include
Family, Background,
and Health.

Give examples for
each, such as:

Family —
Does it make a
difference if he's
happily married?

Background —
Is there a difference
between the person
who was raised on a
farm and one who
lived in a city?

Health —
Suppose he's going
to have an operation?

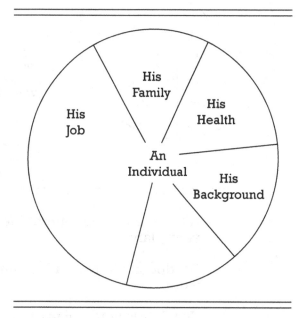

You may also get Recreation, Wages, Love Affairs, Education.

Write down not more than two or three of these.

Leave one segment for other factors.

There are, of course, many additional things which affect the individual on the job.

Leave one section unlabeled.

Let's let this segment represent Other Factors.

The completed chart work will look like this:

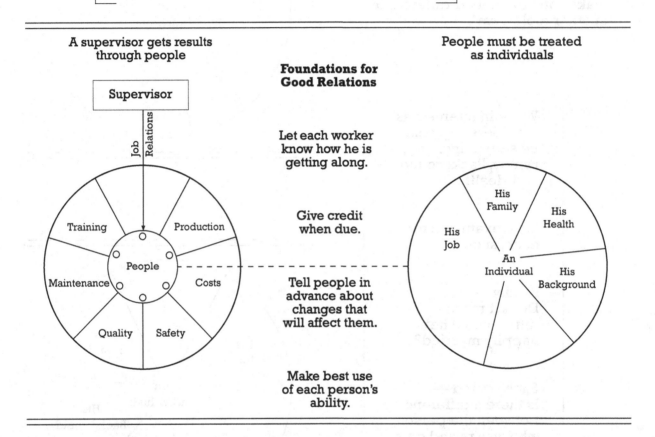

A supervisor gets results through people

Foundations for Good Relations

People must be treated as individuals

Supervisor

Job Relations

Training

Production

People

Maintenance

Costs

Quality

Safety

Let each worker know how he is getting along.

Give credit when due.

Tell people in advance about changes that will affect them.

Make best use of each person's ability.

His Family

His Health

His Job

An Individual

His Background

All of these really affect the individual who comes to work in your plant.

He doesn't leave part of himself at home when he comes to work.

The things noted in the circle make individuals different.

You need to know this person as a separate individual because he is different and that affects him on the job.

These differences are not ones that supervisors can change, but we must recognize them as differences which affect the worker on the job.

Summarize chart:

- A supervisor gets results through people.

- By using the foundations we can improve our relations with people.

- A supervisor must treat his people as individuals.

These are the basis for good job relations.

But their use will not prevent all problems.

DEFINE A "PROBLEM"

What do we mean by a problem?

★ A problem is ANYTHING THE SUPERVISOR
★ *HAS TO TAKE ACTION ON.*

Changes, interruptions, and failures *do* occur; and situations do arise. These cause problems.

Each supervisor needs *skill* in understanding individuals, sizing up situations, and working with people.

We are going to get experience in using a *method* for meeting problems. This method has been developed in sound industrial practice.

What we are going to be working on is the relation between you and the people you supervise.

This relationship is the same whether you are working on a quality problem or a maintenance problem or any of your other responsibilities.

We will consider your responsibilities for production, quality, etc., only in so far as *they are* affected by job relations.

These relations are important.

They affect the job.

Good relations give you good results.

Poor relationships give you poor results.

Conditions change all the time—so do relations.

INTRODUCE T.W.I. METHOD

Tell the problem of Joe Smith.
Do not read. The trainer must be able to *tell* this well, changing no ideas, but using words natural to him.

1. Let us take a look at how one supervisor took action on one of his problems—something that happened in a war production plant.

Joe Smith was a good worker and his earnings were high. The department was busy and was on a regular 6-day schedule. Some time ago Joe had fallen into the habit of laying off every *Monday*. The rush of work was so great that his staying away held up a lot of work. The supervisor had spoken to Joe about it several times—but Joe just said that he was making more money in five days than he used to make in two weeks. The supervisor tried to appeal to Joe's patriotism, but saw that he did not get any place.

Then Joe got married and he started working six days regularly. The supervisor decided that the extra money looked good to Joe and that was why he came to work all the time. Joe kept up the good record for a few months.

Then one Monday a general increase was announced. On Tuesday Joe failed to come to work. The supervisor decided that the extra money had again brought Joe to the place where he could get along on five days' pay. He decided that he was going to teach Joe a lesson, and that the only way to get at Joe was to show him how it would feel to lose five days' pay.

When Joe came in Wednesday, the supervisor was waiting for him on his way to the locker room and called out—"Hey, Joe, don't bother changing. I'm laying you off for a week. That will give you a chance to think over what's in your pay envelope. Maybe you'll decide it won't be so bad to get six days' pay next time."

Erase charts from board.

2. Discuss.

This supervisor had a problem, didn't he?

How do you think he handled it?

★ Just what was this supervisor trying to accomplish?

Get the group to say:

He wanted Joe at work regularly.

If the group tends to agree with the supervisor, remind them that what he wanted was "Joe on the job."

But he sent him home.

Would you have taken this action?

> Do not let this go into extensive discussion.

> If these points do not come out in the discussion, make them yourself:

He made no attempt to find out why Joe didn't come to work that particular day.

The supervisor jumped to the conclusion that Joe, in spite of his apparent change, was after all just an irresponsible person.

That the contents of the pay envelope were all that mattered.

The disciplinary action that the supervisor took was hard on the department.

3. Tell what happened next.

Well—the supervisor laid Joe off. A few days later, at lunch, another supervisor came up to him and said he'd heard he was pretty tough on Joe Smith. Joe's father had been hurt in an accident last Tuesday. Joe had asked the next-door neighbor to send word to the plant that he was called out of town. The neighbor forgot. When Joe went back to the plant Wednesday, he didn't know that his supervisor hadn't heard about what had happened.

4. Discuss.

Do these additional facts throw more light?

Joe had had a good record for a while, but the supervisor had decided that the wage increase was the reason for his not coming to work.

The supervisor felt that he wasn't going to be able to count on him.

Joe's failure to come to work had been for a good reason.

He thought his supervisor had been notified.

Let's look at what the supervisor did from three angles:

How would Joe feel toward his supervisor?

How did the other people in the department feel about the way he treated Joe?

What did it do to production?

It was the wrong thing to do on all three counts.

5. Is there a way to avoid mistakes like this?

What could Joe's supervisor have done first?

If someone suggests "Talk to Joe" or "Give him a chance to explain," ask, "Do you mean 'Get the facts'?"

Write on board: **Get the Facts**

It certainly is important to "*Be sure you have the whole story.*"

Then what would he do with these facts?

Get group to say and write on board: **Weigh and Decide**

Aren't we all tempted to jump to conclusions?

After deciding, what would he do next?

Get group to say and write on board: **Take Action**

It's easy to pass the buck, isn't it?

After you take action, is it a good idea to see how it came out?

Write on board: **Check Results**

Did Joe's supervisor's action help production?

Leave steps on board.

HAND OUT CARDS, SUMMARIZE 4-STEP METHOD

Distribute cards individually—STRESS THEIR IMPORTANCE.

Read the "How to Handle a Problem" and comment as follows:

★ 1. Get the Facts.

We said that Joe's supervisor did not get the facts.

★ Review the record (source of facts).

The supervisor recalled Joe's previous bad record but evidently overlooked his recent good record.

All records are not paper records. You include what you know about someone.

★ Find out what rules and plant customs apply (source of facts).

It apparently was a custom in this plant to call in if you were not coming to work.

There are some things that are accepted as what you do in the plant. Some are written and they're rules. But the unwritten customs are just as strong.

★ Talk with individuals concerned (source of facts)

Joe's supervisor did not take the time to do this.

★ Get opinions and feelings (source of facts).

This supervisor just didn't think of what Joe felt; remember that what a person feels or thinks, right or wrong, is a fact to him and must be considered as such.

★ Be sure you have the whole story (a caution).

You pointed out that the supervisor didn't have the whole story—he did not know *why* Joe didn't come to work.

★ 2. Weigh and Decide.

★ Fit the facts together.

Look for gaps and contradictions. In this one there were gaps, but the supervisor didn't try to fill them in. Joe's father's being hurt is the big gap in the facts.

★ Consider their bearing on each other.

This supervisor only looked at the bearing of some facts on each other. He overlooked Joe's current good record and decided that the wage increase and Joe's previous record accounted for his absence.

★ What possible actions are there?

This supervisor thought there was only one thing to do. There is usually more than one possible action if we stop to weigh all the facts.

★ Check practices and policies.

The supervisor has to know the ground rules. He has to know whether his action is within company policies and practices.

★ Consider objective and effect on individual, group, and production.

Joe's supervisor did not consider the effect of his action on his objective, on Joe, on the other people, or on production.

★ Don't jump to conclusions (a caution).

Do you think that Joe's supervisor jumped to a conclusion?

★ 3. Take Action.

★ Are you going to handle this yourself?

It was up to Joe's supervisor to handle this problem.

★ Do you need help in handling?

Sometimes we can get help from another department—from the plant hospital, personnel, or the payroll department.

★ Should you refer this to your supervisor?

You have to decide whether a problem is beyond your own authority for action.

★ Watch the timing of your action.

The timing does influence the effectiveness of what you do.

★ Don't pass the buck (a caution).

I guess we all know what this means—and we can

say for Joe's supervisor that he didn't pass the buck.

★ 4. Check Results.

It is always important to consider how you are going to follow up.

★ How soon will you follow up?

You make your first check as soon as you can reasonably expect results.

★ How often will you need to check?

Sometimes you keep an eye on something for quite a while just to make sure that your action hasn't caused another problem.

★ Watch for changes in output, attitudes, and relationships.

You have to look at what your action did to the group as well as to the individual person concerned.

★ Did your action help production?

We've seen that Joe's supervisor fell down straight through because:

- he failed to get the facts
- he didn't even consider all the facts he had
- his action was wrong
- and he got poor results

> Ask supervisors to turn the cards over. Read "Foundations for Good Relations," commenting follows :

★ Let each worker know how he is getting along.

Do we all want to know how we are doing?

★ Figure out what you expect of him (action point).

Is it a good idea to decide what he is supposed to do so you can let him know how he is doing?

★ Point out ways to improve (action point).

Does it help much to say "You're all wrong there"?

How about saying "Suppose we try this"?

★ <u>Give credit when due.</u>

Don't we all respond to recognition?

★ <u>Look for extra or unusual performance</u> (action point).

Sometimes it's the man who's unusually reliable who deserves some form of credit.

★ <u>Tell him while "it's hot"</u> (action point).

Don't get so busy that you overlook some simple thanks right when they are due.

★ <u>Tell people in advance about changes that will affect them.</u>

All of us have to get used to changes.

★ <u>Tell them why if possible</u> (action point).

Give reasons, not arbitrary decisions.

★ <u>Get them to accept the change</u> (action point).

Help people to understand.

★ <u>Make best use of each person's ability.</u>

This is particularly important in wartime.

★ <u>Look for ability not currently being used</u> (action point).

Are you sure you know just what skills there are in your shop? Are you training new men when there is a skilled man doing some other job?

★ <u>Never stand in a man's way</u> (action point)

Do people think you hold them back just to get your job done?

★ These are the basic rules for good relations. They will
★ do a job for you if you use them. If they are used they
★ will keep many problems from coming up.

Remember that you need to treat all people as individuals.

These foundations will smooth job relations but they will not insure you against problems.

We have supervisors because there are problems to handle.

You and I are supervisors because management expects us to handle these problems.

SUMMARIZE

1. Good supervision includes two points:

Handling the department and working with the individuals in it in a way which makes everyday relationships smooth and prevents many problems. This is covered by the Foundations.

Handling problems that do arise is covered by the 4-step method.

2. The supervisory job can't be run from a set of rules any more than you can learn to play baseball from a book. You can read about pitching a curve, but you can't get the ball to curve until you have practiced.

3. Conditions *do* change; interruptions do occur; problems do come up. The Foundations and this 4-step method will help you to handle these problems. This is a pattern to follow.

This method applies whether there is a Wagner Act or not, whether you are dealing with a man or a woman, negro or white, Republican or Democrat.

Why is this so? Because *people are people* once you get under their skins, regardless of race or color.

DISCUSS HOW PROBLEMS COME UP

★ Let's look at the way PROBLEMS come up.

★ 1. If you're on the watch in your department you'll be
★ tipped off when you notice changes in people's work or
★ attitudes. Suppose a man suddenly gets quarrelsome
★ with everyone around him—that's a problem, isn't it?
★ Effective supervisors get in on these early.

★ 2. Or, you may even have a situation to *size up before it*
★ *happens.* Management may announce changes in policy.
★ Suppose you are going to bring a group of women into
★ a department where there have been only men. You may
★ want to do some preventive work and size up that situation
★ in advance so that you won't have a problem to handle later.

★ 3. Sometimes they "come to you." A man may ask for a raise
★ or a transfer, or he may have a question about a problem.

★ 4. Others, you "run into." Suppose you tell someone to do
★ something, and he won't do it. Or perhaps it's someone
★ who's late.

CONSIDER SUPERVISOR'S PROBLEMS ON THE JOB

1. ⌐ Distribute problem sheets. ⌐

Some of the same problems come to all supervisors.

Maybe you have all of these—or none.

⌐ Ask group to check problem sheets. ⌐

⌐ Read five or six out loud—discuss, though not at length. ⌐

⌐ Let the group read all the way through. ⌐

In this group we are going to be working on supervisors' problems—the things he has to do something about.

Comment on number of problems group has.

2. ⌐ Describe practice in following sessions.
    See Tips for Trainers. ⌐

Each of you will have a chance to bring in a problem during these sessions.

We will work on these problems to develop our skill in the use of the 4-step method.

JOB RELATIONS SITUATIONS AND PROBLEMS

Lack of teamwork in a department.
Worker doesn't understand his part in the whole job.
Man goes to your boss to complain.
Someone kicks (complains) about working conditions.
Prospective change in hours is apt to make trouble.

Man wants to change jobs often.
Man takes chances at work.
Worker fails to come to work every day.
Employee loses interest in job.
Man feels he is being pushed.

Man resents changes.
Drop in individual production.
Drop in overall production.
Worker irritable and touchy.
Employee kicks (complains) when not promoted.

Plant protection regulations are going to be stiffened.
Worker wants more money.
Employee makes mistakes.
Operator refuses to do certain work.
Employees are not going to get an expected bonus.

Careless with materials and equipment.
Man gets discouraged learning the job.
Time-clock rules are going to be enforced.
Worker wants transfer for more money.
Friction between shifts.

Pay differential causes trouble.
Some day-work jobs are going to be put on piece-rate.
Man loafing on job.
Doesn't like responsibility.
Plant is going to start hiring women, or negroes.

We *are not* going to criticize the supervisor or pass judgment on his action.

When you bring in your problem,

REMEMBER:

★ Our definition of a problem is something the supervisor
★ has to take action on. This includes recommending action.

★ It must involve you and the people you supervise—other-
★ wise we may not have all the facts or know the individuals
★ concerned.

★ You may bring in a problem that you have handled recently.
★ These problems are good because the facts are easily
★ recalled.

★ You may bring in a problem on which you have not as yet
★ taken action. Pending problems are always good.

★ You will help all of us if you will bring some problems that
★ didn't turn out quite right, so we can take a look at why
★ they turned out the way they did.

Please do not bring in as a problem the most involved problem that you have run into in all of your years of supervisory experience. When problems are pretty big, or involved, most of us usually say, "This is a pretty tough one. I'd better get the facts and weigh them carefully."

Supervisors tell us that they usually go a bit sour with the smaller problems, as they appear to be so insignificant that they are prone not to get the facts, jump to conclusions, etc.

We want to get experience and practice here so that we will instinctively think through small problems, so that these small problems will be handled satisfactorily and forgotten.

Some supervisors say that most all of their large problems result from small problems which were poorly handled. If there is a little blaze, we usually can put it out with a cup of water, but if it develops into a big blaze, then we have to call out the Fire Departments from neighboring towns.

Sometimes we overlook the little things. You give someone work to do and he just doesn't do it.

You have a girl who doesn't get to work on time.

These small incidents are problems.

Because of our time limit we have to have short and relatively simple problems. This is necessary because we are going to apply the entire method, not just the beginning of it. We can learn the method just as well on short problems as on long ones. If we get practice and form a habit, it will be easier to use the method on more involved problems, and it will make the handling of those problems shorter.

Remember that the supervisor does much preventive work by handling his problems while they are new and small, rather than waiting until they are older and more complicated.

3. Do any of you have any problems, like these on the problem sheet perhaps, facing you? I mean some you have to handle yourself? Well, will you ....and ....tell us about one at the next meeting, just as I told you about Joe Smith, so we all can take a look at them together?

> Explain procedure for handling supervisor's problems.

4. I'm going to bring in a problem too.

Our purpose in all these problems is to *get practice* in the use of the *4-step method*. We only acquire skill through practice.

5. You can begin to use these foundations and the 4 steps right away—on the job.

That's where this plan pays dividends.

> Thank group for interest and participation.

> Clear the board.

JOB RELATIONS – SESSION II

IMPORTANCE OF GETTING THE FACTS

REVIEW 4-STEP METHOD

> 1. Briefly make appropriate opening comments.

Let's take a look at our 4-step method of handling problems.

2. What are the four steps a good supervisor follows when he takes action on a problem?

> Draw from group and place in upper right hand corner of board:

> 1. Get the Facts
> 2. Weigh and Decide
> 3. Take Action
> 4. Check Results

3. We are setting up a pattern here. We handle these situations in slow motion, in order to get a closer look at them. Actually, on the job, even though this method is many times sped up, you still go through the same steps.

4. This may seem to take time—but if it saves time in the long run, isn't it surely worth it?

DEVELOP ABILITY IN USING THE METHOD by presenting and discussing the Tom problem

> 1. Focus attention on importance of Step 1—Get the Facts.

In the use of this method Step 1 is basic, because the success of Steps 2, 3, and 4, depends on getting all the facts.

> Underline Step 1

> ## 1. Get the Facts

In some problems, ALL THE FACTS are not obtained until personal opinions and feelings are considered. These personal opinions and feelings must be considered as facts. What a worker thinks—right or wrong—is a fact to him and must be considered as such.

I am now going to tell you about a problem in which a supervisor talked with a man and, by getting his opinions and feelings, obtained important facts.

The purpose in relating this particular problem is to stress not only the importance of getting the facts, but also to give us an opportunity to see exactly how this supervisor talked with this man in order to get personal opinions and feelings.

This problem is one where what is said and how it is said is very important. I'm going to read this to you, so we'll get just what was said by both of them.

2. | Read the problem. MAKE IT LIVE. DO NOT READ IN A MONOTONE.

A supervisor is out in the shop and notices a workman is reaching into a machine.

Supervisor calls out: Tom, I've told you to shut off that machine when you take off the guard.

| Trainer Comment: The supervisor is mad. He's apparently warned Tom before.

Tom yells back: If you want to fire me, why don't you say so instead of nagging at me all the time.

| Trainer Comment: Tom is mad, too.

Supervisor: Keep your shirt on! It's far from firing you, Tom. I just don't want you to fire yourself by getting your hand mashed. The number of times that machine has to be adjusted makes me think there must be something wrong with it.

Tom: Well, I'm not going to take any more panning.

| Trainer Comment: The supervisor is certainly facing a problem and here is what went through his mind very quickly before he took any action.

Supervisor: Now, let's see. I've known Tom a long time. He's been one of the best men in the department. He says I've been nagging him. He is reckless as the devil about his machine. Yesterday I had to call him on quality. And it hasn't been so long since I had to tell him that his line wasn't keeping up with the rest. What's happened to Tom? I guess I have been on his neck a lot. But it was always something that had to be done. And I can't have him taking chances the way he does.

> Trainer Comment: Do you notice how this problem came up? There had been a change in Tom, but the supervisor didn't get into the problem then. He waited until it burst in his face.

Supervisor: Suppose we get together this afternoon and talk this over. I'll let you know when I can get someone to relieve you.

> Trainer Comment: Why do you think the supervisor didn't talk to him then? Do you think it would have done any good to stay there right then and *argue* with him? He isn't going to talk in the department or while Tom is mad.

That afternoon Tom comes into the supervisor's office.

Supervisor: Hello, Tom. Sit down. Now, Tom, I guess you think I've been riding you. I don't want to do anything like that. A couple of times I felt I *had* to stop you because you were doing something dangerous. And there have been a couple of times lately when your work hasn't been quite up to par. I'm used to quality work and plenty of it from you.

Every time I see you taking a chance that might cause trouble, I've got to stop you. When your work isn't up to standard, why then I've got to say something about that too.

Now is there something the matter with the machine? I know you're always raising the guard and reaching into it. If there's something wrong with that machine, I want to get it fixed.

> Trainer Comment: What is the supervisor doing here? The supervisor is trying the obvious thing first—to see if the trouble is connected with the machine.

Tom: Well, if you think I'm going to run over to that switch and pull it, and hang the "don't touch" sign on it—you're just crazy. You're yelling now about how little I get done. If I had to spend half of my time turning that switch off and on, I wouldn't get anything done. And the other day you said the parts were below standard. Well, if I didn't fix that machine they'd all be below standard.

> Trainer Comment: Tom isn't going to make it easy, is he? The supervisor could have cut in there and told him it wouldn't take half the time to turn off the switch. Here again he could have *argued*, but he had gotten Tom in there because he wanted to talk with him, so he wasn't going to *interrupt* him.

Supervisor: Now, Tom, there's more to it than breaking a safety rule. There's a reason behind that rule. You're apt to get your hand mashed.

Tom: And that'd cost the company money, wouldn't it?

> Trainer Comment: The supervisor might think that Tom was sore at the company about money—or would that be *jumping to a conclusion?*

Supervisor: Oh, sure it would cost the company money. But have we made you think that's all we're interested in?

Tom: Well, that's all that counts with some people.

> Trainer Comment: (He's bitter about something.)

Supervisor: It'd cost us a good man. And that's a harder thing to replace than money.

Tom: Well, not everybody feels that way.

> Trainer Comment: He seems to be thinking about the *importance* of money to *some* people. The supervisor has a cue here—will he follow it up? Tom has been pretty hard to talk to. What does the supervisor have to follow up from here?
>
> Do not allow extended discussion. If the group does not make the point, say that Tom seems to be thinking about the importance of money to somebody.

Supervisor: Why are you so strong on the money angle? You're doing all right that way, aren't you? Seems to me you told me last spring you were going to build on that land of yours out on the pike. When are you getting married? When you have a wife she won't want you to take chances.

Tom: Oh—nobody cares if I do get a hand cut off.

Supervisor: Your girl would care.

Tom: I don't have a girl any more.

Supervisor: I'm sorry, Tom. I just wanted to get you thinking of what an injury to you might mean to somebody else.

Tom: Well, it doesn't mean anything to anyone now. Nothing about me would hurt her. Why, she knew I was going to start to build, but she married someone else. So, all I have is a half-finished house. And that's all I've got to show for it.

Nobody cares what happens to me any more. And I don't need to try to make any more money, or save it either. It changes a lot of things.

> Trainer Comment: This takes careful handling. The supervisor wants to get Tom back to normal production; he wants to stay on good terms with Tom. Now the supervisor has a chance to make a speech—he could tell Tom he was lucky to get rid of her, but he's going to listen to Tom, and *not do all the talking himself.*

Supervisor: A blow like that's bad, and it's no use saying it isn't. But sometimes you just have to take it on the chin. Some things can be fixed up, though. And I wish you'd see your way clear to helping me figure out what's wrong with the way that line is running.

I can see why you have gotten a bit careless about taking chances. But I know you wouldn't have had to take those chances unless something else had been wrong. Now, is the machine worn? Does it need overhauling? How are the tools?

> Trainer Comment: There seem to be *two* things to look at: (1) the man and (2) the machine.

Tom: No, it isn't the machine. The parts aren't coming through the same as they used to. There's a burr left on them; and after so many have gone through, well, I just have to clean the machine out.

> Handle this problem according to standard procedure.

3. Just what is Tom's supervisor trying to accomplish?

> Get from group and place on board:

To make Tom a safe worker and get production back to normal

4. What are the facts?

> Get facts from group and put on board briefly. See that these are included, but not necessarily in this order.

Facts

Was a good worker
Quality and quantity down
Broke safety rule
Careless
Warned before
Talked back
Lost his girl
Felt nobody cared
Burrs on parts

> Check subheads of Step 1. USE CARD.

> Be sure that you leave group with the realization that the supervisor got three very important facts because he talked with the individual to get their opinions and feelings.

5. Consider Step 2, according to standard procedure.

| Get possible actions from group. Some may be — Warn about safety rules. Give penalty layoff. Report bad parts. Tell him losing girl isn't your fault. | **Weigh and decide** **Possible Actions** _____ _____ _____ |

> Test possible actions against objective and probable effect on individual—group—production.

6. Now let us see what did happen in this particular problem.

> Continue to read the problem.

Supervisor: I can see why that would cause you trouble. Suppose we go down and take a look at those parts. Now, I'm sorry about your tough luck. But I do thank you for helping me.

> Trainer Comment: Throughout, the supervisor had listened sympathetically to Tom, he had encouraged and helped him to talk about the things that were important to him. Now that he had reached something specific, bad parts, he's going to check that.
>
> Later the supervisor comes back to his office and calls his own chief.

Supervisor: Jones, can I come up a minute? I want to talk to you about the parts we're getting from the punch press department. They're not coming through clean. I have a good operator on our line, and it's interfering with his work and slowing down our output.

7. What were the additional facts that Tom's supervisor got by talking with Tom and getting his opinions and feelings?

> Point out on board THE ADDITIONAL FACTS:

> Lost his girl
> Felt nobody cared
> Burrs on parts

8. The supervisor looked at all the facts and he felt he had a complete story.

He found out why Tom was off the beam.

Doesn't this indicate that sometimes an addition of one more fact will preclude or suggest a possible action? Do you think we would have had the same possible actions if these facts had been missing?

9. What action did he take?

> Help group give supervisor's action. Write this action on the board:

> ### ACTION
>
> Told Tom he was sorry
> Asked Tom's help
> Checked parts
> Reported faulty parts

What facts did this supervisor use in arriving at this decision?

> Handle Step 3 as in the standard procedure.

Let's look at Step 3.

Are you going to handle this yourself?

> It was this supervisor's problem.

> He had some responsibility to take some action.

Need help?

> Yes, he got Tom's help—no outside help necessary.

Refer to supervisor?

> To get good parts—but didn't tell him Tom's trouble.

Timing?

> Tom's supervisor didn't lose any time in acting.

10. Handle Step 4 as in the standard procedure.

How soon do you think he'll follow up? More than once?

What will he look for?

Do you think Tom's supervisor will accomplish his objective?

Did this supervisor use the 4-step method up to now?

11. Conclusion to the Tom Problem.

You remember the purpose of this problem was to stress not only the importance of getting the facts, but also to see how this supervisor handled this problem in order to get personal opinions and feelings. You can see what might have happened if this supervisor had not decided to get more facts before he took his action.

Do you think Tom's supervisor was justified in getting him to talk about his personal affairs? This depends on the individual and the problem. This supervisor knew his individual well enough to talk with Tom.

Did *you* ever have a man go sour when something happened in his family? He brought what happened outside of work into the plant with him just as Tom did. That's why the supervisor has to concern himself with personal feelings.

45 min
to here

Did you notice that when Tom's supervisor called his boss he didn't reveal the personal information he had about Tom? He could have said, "I have a jilted guy down here," but he said, "I have a good worker down here."

Clear board, except steps.

REMEMBER WE SAID THAT OPINIONS AND FEELINGS are hard to get

We all can learn and develop this skill. Once this skill is acquired it becomes a useful tool for a supervisor.

Write on board:

How to get opinions and feelings

1. Just how did Tom's supervisor find out about Tom's opinions and feelings?

His supervisor could have argued with Tom about its taking him half his time to turn off the switch. Is anything ever satisfactorily settled by an argument? Our first tip, then, is "Don't argue."

> Write on board:

Don't argue

2. It took some encouragement to get Tom to talk about what seemed important to him, didn't it? The supervisor had to help him say what was wrong. The tip then is to, "Encourage him to talk about what is important to him."

> Write on board:

Encourage him to talk about what is important to him

3. If you are telling a story and someone interrupts you, do you feel like continuing it? After Tom started talking did his boss interrupt him? Our tip is "Don't interrupt."

> Write on board:

Don't interrupt

4. Could the boss have spoiled everything by jumping to the conclusion that Tom was sore about money? The tip is, "Don't jump to conclusions."

> Write on board:

Don't jump to conclusions

5. The supervisor had a chance to make a couple of speeches, didn't he—on safety—on how lucky he was to get rid of the girl? You will notice he didn't do all the talking himself. The tip is "Don't do all the talking yourself."

> Write on board:

Don't do all the talking yourself

6. Was Tom's boss a good listener? If you want to get opinions and feelings you have to listen, don't you? Our tip is, "Listen."

> Write on board:

Listen

> Bring out to the group the importance of using these tips.

Clear Board—except Question and Steps.

Change question to "this supervisor" in place of "Tom's supervisor."

SUPERVISORS' PROBLEMS

Handle 2 problems.
35 minutes each.
Standard Procedure.

MAKE SURE 3 PROBLEMS WILL BE PRESENTED AT NEXT SESSION

1. I'll bring in another problem at the next session.

2. Will all of you have one ready?

Now you can bring in a problem you want to size up to try to take some preventive action.

Or you can bring one that's on your hands right now.

Or perhaps you have just finished a problem we can consider.

But we do set up these requirements:

★ It must be something between you and the people
★ you supervise.

★ It must be a problem which you have to handle;
★ not someone else's job.

★ You must have the necessary information about the
★ employee or employees involved—age, length of
★ service, experience, etc.

.... and .... brought in the kind of problems we have to live with. That's the kind we want.

3. Do all of you have a problem that you can tell us about? To practice our 4-step method?

If any member of group says he does not have a problem, use the problem sheet again.

Remind the group that, in order to receive a certificate, each member must bring in a problem, participate satisfactorily, and attend all sessions.

Clear the board.

Just what is Tom's
supervisor trying
to accomplish?

To make Tom a safe
worker and get
production back to
normal.

Facts

Was a good worker
Quality and quantity down
Broke safety rule
Careless
Warned before
Talked back
Lost his girl
Felt nobody cared
Burrs on parts

1. Get the Facts
2. Weigh and Decide
3. Take Action
4. Check Results

Weigh and Decide

Possible Actions

Warn about safety rules
Give penalty layoff
Report bad parts
Tell him losing girl isn't
  your fault

ACTION

Told Tom he was sorry
Asked Tom's help
Checked parts
Reported faulty parts

STANDARD PROCEDURE

1. Ask supervisor to tell problem.

Head of table. Does this involve you and somebody who comes under your direction?

2. How problems come up.

Where appropriate, stress; you sensed, or anticipated a change.

3. Get objective.

Get from supervisor:
Something to shoot at. May be changed.
What do you want to have happen here?
Does this problem affect the group?
What net result do you want after you have taken action?
Get group agreement.

4. Get Facts.

Supervisor first, as he recalls them offhand.
Review subheads with supervisor—USE CARDS.
Get additional facts from group—USE CARDS.

5. Weigh and Decide.

Fit facts—Look for gaps and contradictions with group.
Possible Action:
What facts used?—From contributor.
Check practices and policies with supervisor.
Check objective first with group, then last with supervisor.
Check probable effect on individual, group, and production, with supervisor.

6. Balance of Case.

Facts used (from supervisor).

7. Check Step 3.

Subheads—with supervisor.
Why?—How?—Timing?

8. Check Step 4.

Subheads—with supervisor.
When?—How often?—What?

9. Check Objective.

Supervisor.

10. Foundations (if applicable)

Supervisor.

(Thank Supervisor and clear board except questions and steps.)

WEIGHING AND DECIDING

Before session starts, place on board:	Just what is this supervisor trying to accomplish?	1. Get the Facts 2. Weigh and Decide 3. Take Action 4. Check Results

Time Table Allow 5 min

REVIEW 4-STEP METHOD

1. Now, do we all have our cards? Suppose we take a look at the 4-step method. In our last session the problem I presented about Tom, who lost his girl, stressed the importance of getting the facts, with particular reference to personal opinions and feelings.

We looked at the way a supervisor got the facts in order to make a good decision. It takes time to do this, but in the long run it does save time, doesn't it?

2. It is interesting to notice that a similar method is used by professional people. For instance, let us see how a doctor handles his problem.

Step 1—Does the doctor get the facts?

Record personal history—blood pressure—temperature.

Rules and customs—medical knowledge—practice—ethics.

Talk—to get more facts, confidential.

Opinions and feelings—very important.

Step 2—Diagnosis.

Fit facts together—assemble facts.

Consider bearing on each other—symptoms.

Possible actions—medicine, operate.

Check practices and policies—must comply with laws.

Effect on individual—group—contagion.

Don't jump to conclusions—careful diagnosis.

Step 3—Treatment.

Take action—prescribe, operate.

Handle yourself?—his specialty.

Help in handling—nurse, technician.

Refer to supervisor—more experienced doctor, specialist.

Doctors don't lose face in doing this.

Timing—importance of timing.

Don't pass the buck.

Step 4—Check results—X-ray.

How soon—depends on case.

How often—it differs.

Watch for—changes in condition.

This method we have been talking about works in other professions, doesn't it? The doctor in an emergency of life or death still takes time for all these steps.

3. Now let's turn the spotlight on Step 2 of our method, Weigh and Decide.

Good decisions must have a good foundation. You must have the facts.

They must be weighed.

| Underline Step 2. |

2. Weigh and decide

PRESENT THE SHIPYARD PROBLEM

1. Let's take a look at something that happened in a shipyard, and particularly at the decision the supervisor made since we are today stressing Step 2.

| Tell the opening of the problem. |

The electrical shop supervisor in a shipyard told a man to get some tools. The man said he couldn't—he'd left his checks at home. So the supervisor reminded him he could get them by signing for them—the man refused, said he didn't like it in the shop anyway, and he wanted to go back to outside work. The supervisor was pretty sore about the man's refusal to get the tools.

This man was an oldtimer. He had always been on outside work, but he had hurt his foot. So, as soon as he was able to fill a job in the shop, he was transferred into the shop at the same rate, that way he could get full pay instead of part-time pay under workmen's compensation. His foot had been healed for some time and he had asked when he was going back to his outside job. But the shop was busy, so the supervisor kept the man. He had been uncooperative ever since he came into the shop; now he flatly refused to do some work. People in the department were watching to see how it would come out.

The supervisor decided it was time to take action.

2. Comment on how problem came up—ran into, but supervisor had warning—oldtimer uncooperative in shop.

3. Get the objective from group and put on board:

Get the job done without upsetting the department

4. Continue with standard procedure to get these facts, but not necessarily in this order. Place on board.

Facts

Oldtimer
Foot hurt
Inside for full pay
Foot healed
Asked transfer outside
Shop busy
Uncooperative inside
Refused to get tools
Department watching
Supervisor sore

Review the card, subheads Step 1

5. STEP 2—FOLLOW STANDARD PROCEDURE.

Get possible actions from group. Some may be:

Layoff
Transfer
Fire

Weigh and decide

Possible Actions

Test possible actions against objective and probable effect on individual—group—and production.

6. Now let's finish the problem and see what actually happened.

The supervisor fired the oldtimer. The oldtimer protested to the union and his case was taken up. The union proceeded to get additional facts which could have been obtained by the supervisor.

The oldtimer had almost twenty years of satisfactory service out in the yard. He liked to work outside, although it meant being out in all kinds of weather. He did not like shop work. He did not know that he had been brought into the shop to increase his earnings over what he would have received from compensation. The yard supervisor was not even questioned about the man's long service outside.

Eventually the workman was reinstated in the yard, on his old job with back pay.

7. Get additional facts from group and list on board under facts.

Facts

Long O.K. service outside
Liked outside work
Not advised why inside — pay

8. Continue with standard procedure.

Write on the blackboard:

ACTION

Fired oldtimer

Have group identify the facts which the oldtimer's supervisor used when he came to the decision of firing the oldtimer.

Also have group identify the facts which were not used by the oldtimer's supervisor in making this decision.

Does this make a reasonable case for the oldtimer?

Does this indicate to you that, if the supervisor had intelligently weighed all the facts which he had, he would not have fired the oldtimer?

Stress to the group that the supervisor gave weight to only a very few of the facts which he had as a basis for his decision.

Other supervisors, by giving more weight to the facts which he missed, might arrive at other decisions, such as those already listed on the blackboard under Possible Actions.

9. Comment on Step 3 subheads—Standard Procedure. Have group follow cards.

Handle yourself?—This was his problem.

Help in handling?—Didn't ask for help.

Refer to supervisor?—Didn't refer to boss.

Timing of action?—Was this the time to take action?

10. Comment on Step 4 subheads—Standard Procedure. Use cards.

How soon? How often?

This supervisor did not check up on the results of his action. He evidently thought that when he fired the old-timer the problem was solved.

Changes in attitudes and relationships?

This supervisor lost standing with the individual, the group, and his management.

11. Check objective.

12. Use foundation points as in standard procedure.

Hit hard on "Tell People In Advance About Changes That Will Affect Them" and "Make Best Use of Each Person's Ability." (Prevention)

13. It is interesting to note in this problem that even though the supervisor did not have all the facts, nevertheless he did not do a good job of weighing the facts which he had.

Perhaps if he had given more weight to several seemingly un-important facts, he would not have taken the action which he did.

Clear the blackboard except question and steps.

SUPERVISORS' PROBLEMS

Handle 3 problems
2 problems 30 min. each
1 problem 25 min.
Standard Procedure

MAKE SURE THREE PROBLEMS WILL BE PRESENTED AT NEXT SESSION

Re-emphasize what you mean by a problem; how they come up. Remind group that, to receive a certificate, each supervisor must bring in a problem, participate satisfactorily, and attend all five sessions.

Clear the board.

Just what is this

supervisor trying

to accomplish?

1. Get the Facts
2. Weigh and Decide
3. Take Action
4. Check Results

To get the job done
without upsetting
the department

Facts

Oldtimer
Foot hurt
Inside for full pay
Foot healed
Asked transfer outside
Shop busy
Uncooperative inside
Refused to get tools
Department watching
Supervisor sore
Long O.K. service outside
Liked outside work
Not advised why inside — pay

Weigh and Decide

Possible Actions

Lay off
Transfer
Fire

ACTION

Fired oldtimer

STANDARD PROCEDURE

1. Ask supervisor to tell problem.

Head of table. Does this involve you and somebody who comes under your direction?

2. How problems come up.

Where appropriate, stress; you sensed, or anticipated a change.

3. Get objective.

Get from supervisor:
Something to shoot at. May be changed.
What do you want to have happen here?
Does this problem affect the group?
What net result do you want after you have taken action?
Get group agreement.

4. Get Facts.

Supervisor first, as he recalls them offhand.
Review subheads with supervisor—USE CARDS.
Get additional facts from group—USE CARDS.

5. Weigh and Decide.

Fit facts—Look for gaps and contradictions with group.
Possible Action:
What facts used?—From contributor.
Check practices and policies with supervisor.
Check objective first with group, then last with supervisor.
Check probable effect on individual, group, and production, with supervisor.

6. Balance of Case.

Facts used (from supervisor).

7. Check Step 3.

Subheads—with supervisor.
Why?—How?—Timing?

8. Check Step 4.

Subheads—with supervisor.
When?—How often?—What?

9. Check Objective.

Supervisor.

10. Foundations (if applicable)

Supervisor.

(Thank Supervisor and clear board except questions and steps.)

TAKING PREVENTIVE ACTION AND CHECKING RESULTS

Before session starts, place on board:	Just what is this supervisor trying to accomplish?	1. Get the Facts 2. Weigh and Decide 3. Take Action 4. Check Results

---

Time Table Allow 35 min

PRACTICE ON STEPS 3 AND 4

1. Make appropriate opening comments.

2. By the use of the Tom problem in Session II we discussed securing the facts through getting personal opinions and feelings.

Using the Oldtimer problem in our last session we practiced on Step 2, "Weigh and Decide."

In this session we are going to hit hard on Steps 3 and 4, "Take Action," and "Check Results."

Underline Steps 3 and 4.

3. Take Action
4. Check Results

Now I am going to present a problem which shows how a supervisor took action which was preventive, and how he checked the results of that action.

3. Because of expansion, scarcity of labor, and many other reasons, changes are taking place in organizations throughout the country.

There are many different types of changes such as:

  change in shift
  change in arrangement of benches or machines

This problem illustrates ONE KIND of change.

4. Tell the opening of the problem of the woman supervisor.

The plant superintendent called Jim White, the General Foreman, into his office and told him that the management had decided to use women supervisors as well as men.

The superintendent told Jim to fill supervisory vacancies with women on the basis of seniority and ability, as was the rule with men.

He also told him that both men and women supervisors were to have the same authority and the same opportunity for advancement. Jim considered this very carefully and reviewed the following facts:

One supervisory position had to be filled, and no qualified men were available. All men capable of supervisory responsibility had been upgraded or had been taken into the armed forces. Most of the new employees who had come to the plant in the last 18 months were women.

Jim selected the best qualified woman for the job. As she was to be the first woman supervisor in the plant, Jim anticipated trouble. This was a major change. Some men supervisors might resent it. Also some men and women employees might not like having a woman in authority. More women supervisors would probably be appointed later.

This was the problem Jim faced.

Should he do anything about it?

5. Discuss how this problem came up—saw it coming.

6. Obtain objective—use standard procedure.

Get from group and place on board:

To get woman supervisor accepted

7. Go through Step 1—Get Facts—Use standard procedure.

Facts

Get facts from group – list on board, but not necessarily in this order.

No women supervisors before
Rule – seniority — ability
Same authority and opportunity
One job open
No qualified men
Woman selected
Anticipated trouble — supervisors, employees

Review the subheads Step 1—Use standard procedure.

8. Go through Step 2—Use standard procedure.

Get possible actions
which group suggests.
They may be:

Mass meeting
Notice on bulletin board
Appoint her—say nothing

Weigh and decide

Possible Actions

_____

_____

_____

9. Check all possible actions against objective, and
probable effect on individual, group, and production.

10. Tell balance of problem.

Jim thought the situation over pretty carefully. Then he talked individually with his supervisors and also he talked individually to those of the operators who were looked on as natural leaders. He gave them the facts and asked for their help.

There was quite a commotion—some people said they wouldn't stand for it. Jim gave them a chance to do their talking and blowing off. Eventually the workers agreed.

By the time the new supervisor took over her work the outburst was over and the people cooperated in accepting her. Before she went into her department Jim talked with her. He told her that she was going to be the first woman supervisor in the plant and that she might run into some difficulty and that she must not be easily offended. He asked her to do her best because it would not only affect her but also other women supervisors who would be appointed later.

During the first day on her new job, Jim talked with the supervisors and, later in the day, with the natural leaders he had talked with before. They informed him that apparently the new supervisor was accepted and everything was O.K. Jim, to be sure that his preventive action was effective, kept in close touch with the situation for some time.

11. Get supervisor's
action from group
and list on board:

ACTION

Gave the facts in advance,
to supervisors – natural
leaders
Asked their help
Let them blow off steam
Asked cooperation of
new supervisor

What facts did Jim consider?

12. Discuss Step 3, TAKE ACTION—Standard Procedure —
Use Cards. Get from group or make the following points
yourself:

Jim handled this himself—why?

> Jim felt it was his job as General Foreman, and he was
> best qualified to handle it.

Did Jim get help? What advantage was it?

> Jim got help from supervisors and natural leaders be-
> cause they were in a position to help him get acceptance
> of the change.

Should Jim have referred this to his supervisor?

> Jim's supervisor had referred it to him.

In what way did Jim's timing contribute to the success of his
action?

> Jim allowed just the right time for them to blow off steam
> and cool off before introducing the woman supervisor.

Could Jim have passed the buck? How?

> Could have blamed management for the idea.

13. Discuss Step 4, CHECK RESULTS. Standard Procedure.
Use Cards.

How soon? Why was it important for Jim to check immediately?

> This change affected the whole plant.

How often? Jim kept in close touch with the situation. Why?

> Jim must check closely until he is certain the change is
> accepted.

Did Jim check effect upon attitudes, relationships, and output?
What did he look for?

> Good attitude of fellow supervisors indicates accep-
> tance of change.

> Good relationship with employees in her department
> proves her acceptance.

Did Jim accomplish his objective? How did he know? He used
Step 4.

14. What foundation points were used in this problem?

Bring out Foundations 3 and 4:

> "Tell people in advance about changes that will affect them."

> "Make best use of each person's ability."

> Clear the board except question and steps.

DISCUSS EFFECT OF CHANGE

Let's take a look at the importance of preparing for the introduction of changes which affect individuals and groups.

> Making that change in Jim's department was something new. Individuals had personal feelings about how this change would affect them.

> People generally get used to doing things in a particular place or in a certain way. We are all inclined to question whether it is necessary to change the things we have become accustomed to.

> Do workers resist changes which affect their work place or tools or the people they will be working with or next to?

> This, then, is a place where one of our foundations for good job relations comes in—tell people in advance about changes that will affect them.

> Preparing the way for a change is surely an equally good thing to do when changes in payment plans, hours, locations of the department, new machinery, new products, or material are about to be introduced.

> The first boy put into a group of oldtimers, or a woman on machines that have always been run by men, are typical of problems supervisors can do something about in advance.

> Preparation of this sort prevents problems from arising later, saves time, and improves relationships.

But even though the way has been prepared for the change, it is still wise to check the results to find out how the individual
or the members of the group accommodate themselves to the change.

Time
Table
Allow
1 hr
25 min

2 hrs
to here

SUPERVISORS' PROBLEMS

Handle 3 problems
2 problems 30 min. each
1 problem 25 min.
Standard Procedure

Clear the board.

Just what is this

supervisor trying

to accomplish?

    To get woman supervisor accepted.

Facts

No women supervisors
    before
Rule — seniority — ability
Same authority and
    opportunity
One job open
No qualified men
Woman selected
Anticipated trouble —
    supervisors, employees

1. Get the Facts
2. Weigh and Decide
3. Take Action
4. Check Results

Weigh and Decide

Possible Actions

    Mass meeting
    Notice on bulletin board
    Appoint her — say nothing

ACTION

Gave the facts in advance,
    to supervisors – natural
    leaders
Asked their help
Let them blow off steam
Asked cooperation of
    new supervisor

STANDARD PROCEDURE

1. Ask supervisor to tell problem.

   Head of table. Does this involve you and somebody who comes under your direction?

2. How problems come up.

   Where appropriate, stress; you sensed, or anticipated a change.

3. Get objective.

   Get from supervisor:
   Something to shoot at. May be changed.
   What do you want to have happen here?
   Does this problem affect the group?
   What net result do you want after you have taken action?
   Get group agreement.

4. Get Facts.

   Supervisor first, as he recalls them offhand.
   Review subheads with supervisor—USE CARDS.
   Get additional facts from group—USE CARDS.

5. Weigh and Decide.

   Fit facts—Look for gaps and contradictions with group.
   Possible Action:
   What facts used?—From contributor.
   Check practices and policies with supervisor.
   Check objective first with group, then last with supervisor.
   Check probable effect on individual, group, and production, with supervisor.

6. Balance of Case.

   Facts used (from supervisor).

7. Check Step 3.

   Subheads—with supervisor.
   Why?—How?—Timing?

8. Check Step 4.

   Subheads—with supervisor.
   When?—How often?—What?

9. Check Objective.

   Supervisor.

10. Foundations (if applicable)

    Supervisor.

(Thank Supervisor and clear board except questions and steps.)

A SUPERVISOR'S OTHER RELATIONSHIPS

Before session starts, place on board:	Just what is this supervisor trying to accomplish?

1. Get the Facts
2. Weigh and Decide
3. Take Action
4. Check Results

Time Table
Allow
50 min

SUPERVISOR'S PROBLEMS

1. Make appropriate opening comments.

50 min to here

2. Handle two problems—25 min. each.

Allow 25 min

1. 25 minutes is allowed here if necessary for the handling of the tenth supervisor's problem, or an additional problem from the group. If this time is not needed, go right on with session.

50 min or 1 hr 15 min to here

THANK GROUP FOR INTEREST AND PARTICIPATION.

Clear board.

Allow 10 min

REVIEW OF JOB RELATIONS CARD

1. Are there any questions about the 4-step method for handling a supervisor's problem?

2. Review foundations for good relations briefly.

All people like to be treated in accord with foundations of good relations. We all can do something about these things. Putting these foundations to work on the job, day by day, will prevent many problems from developing.

Refer to problem sheet.

3. However, when problems do come up, we have a 4-step method to help us handle these problems.

This method will help you get better results, only if you USE it!

4. Review 4-step method including sub-heads, briefly.

5. Review tips for getting personal opinions and feelings. Try to get as many as possible from group.

Put on board:

How to get opinions and feelings

Don't argue
Encourage individuals to talk about what is important to them
Don't interrupt
Don't jump to conclusions
Don't do all the talking yourself
Listen

6. Considering the importance of people in the situation and knowing what is important to the individual person is not a matter of right or wrong or just or unjust. It is simply a common-sense approach to good supervision.

This is one of the hardest parts of the supervisor's job—it may be thought to take too much time, but day-by-day use of this skill of dealing with people will save time in the long run.

The supervisor who knows his people well enough to build them into a smooth operating group is making his important contribution to war production.

Clear Board.

CLINCH ACCEPTANCE OF THE METHOD

by showing advantages to each supervisor

1. What do you think *you* will gain from using this method? How will it help you personally in your department?

Without too much insistence, bring out through discussion and place on board such points as:

More confidence in ability to handle people
Better standing with those you supervise
Better standing with your boss
Fewer headaches
Less Criticism
Organized plan to follow

If necessary, use these questions:

Will this help you to handle some problems yourself— instead of passing them on to the boss?

If you get the whole story before you make decisions, do you think it will improve relationships in your department?

Will it help to have a regular method to follow? How?

Clear the board.

DISCUSS SUPERVISOR'S OTHER RELATIONSHIPS

Show how he is linked to fellow-supervisors, to service and staff departments.

1. Quickly re-develop the "Supervisor's Job" chart from Session I.

Let's go back to the chart we developed in the first session.

Develop on board
the following
supervisory chart:

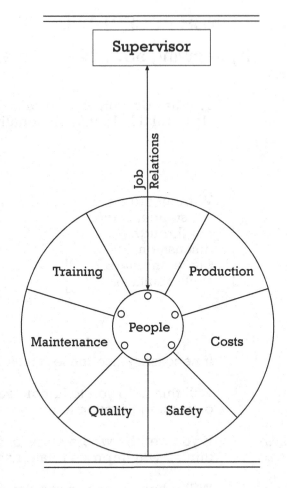

So far we have
been looking at
the supervisor's
relations with
people whose
work he directs.

Is this the only kind
of relationships you
have?

What other people
in the plant do you
work with?

Ask these questions if necessary:

Who gives you your instructions?

Where do your materials come from?

Where does your production go?

What other people do you call on for help?

Do any people who don't work in your department ever
come in it?

Do you work with any union representatives?

These union representatives work with these people
too.

If there is no union, do not use this question or place
"Shop Steward" on the chart.

Add names, boxes, and Job Relations lines.

Each time a Job Relations line is placed on the board, be sure to touch on the fact that this relationship also goes both ways as indicated by the arrowheads.

Also ask "Is this relationship important to the supervisor?" and "Is this relationship important to the whole plant?" The answer in both cases is "Yes."

Then ask "What can he use to assist him in maintaining this strong relationship?" The answer, of course, is "The foundations and 4-step method." This should be brought out from the group.

The completed chart will appear like this:

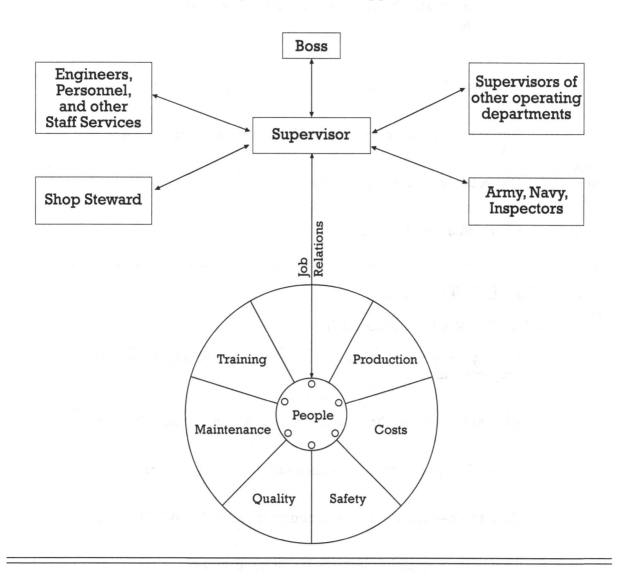

The supervisor is in touch with all these people and departments.

2. We have said that *the supervisor gets results through people*.

Everything you do as a supervisor depends on people. How you get along with people is a measure of your standing.

Does your boss think it's an asset for a supervisor to have the reputation of working well with people?

With all these people it will be a good idea to remember first of all that they are all people and must be treated as individuals.

And we must realize that there is a Job Relations line between the supervisor and all these other people on the chart—and if we are to keep good relations with them we must use these foundation points.

Before you take any action—before you go to another supervisor—or to your boss—you'll want to make certain you've got the facts.

And be sure you have the whole story.

That you "Weigh and Decide" and not jump to conclusions. That you "Take Action" and not pass the buck.

And you'll always come to this final test when you "Check results."

Did your action help production?

Leave chart on board.

CREATE CONVICTION

that each will use this skill

1. Maybe sometimes you wonder whether what *you* do, does help production.

2. Ask each man how many people he supervises *directly*.

Write the figures on the blackboard, beside the chart.

Total them—put the figure in center of chart ABOVE "*People*."

That many people *do* influence war production.

And what *you* do, influences those people.

62

*Time
Table*

3. Emphasize the strategic position of the supervisor —
the supervisor is the officer in the Army of Production.

Everyday relationships count.

*1 hr
35 min
or
2 hrs
to here*

★ 4. We are all working on the same job—turning out war
★ production for the men in the armed forces.

★ We all have one customer—Uncle Sam.

★ One objective—to win the war.

END HERE NO MATTER HOW EARLY.

Clear the board as members of group are leaving.

STANDARD PROCEDURE

1. Ask supervisor to tell problem.

   Head of table. Does this involve you and somebody who comes under your direction?

2. How problems come up.

   Where appropriate, stress; you sensed, or anticipated a change.

3. Get objective.

   Get from supervisor:
   Something to shoot at. May be changed.
   What do you want to have happen here?
   Does this problem affect the group?
   What net result do you want after you have taken action?
   Get group agreement.

4. Get Facts.

   Supervisor first, as he recalls them offhand.
   Review subheads with supervisor—USE CARDS.
   Get additional facts from group—USE CARDS.

5. Weigh and Decide.

   Fit facts—Look for gaps and contradictions with group.
   Possible Action:
   What facts used?—From contributor.
   Check practices and policies with supervisor.
   Check objective first with group, then last with supervisor.
   Check probable effect on individual, group, and production, with supervisor.

6. Balance of Case.

   Facts used (from supervisor).

7. Check Step 3.

   Subheads—with supervisor.
   Why?—How?—Timing?

8. Check Step 4.

   Subheads—with supervisor.
   When?—How often?—What?

9. Check Objective.

   Supervisor.

10. Foundations (if applicable)

   Supervisor.

(Thank Supervisor and clear board except questions and steps.)

Job Relations Reference 1

JOB RELATIONS IN THE FIELD

The following policies and procedures, which are concerned chiefly with quality control of Job Relations, are stated for the Job Relations Trainer's guidance and information.

1. Job Relations is to be put on *exactly* as outlined in the manual.

2. During the first 10-hour program put on by any Job Relations Trainer he will be visited by an Institute Conductor or a Quality Control man for at least one session and preferably two.

3. Each Job Relations Trainer may be visited in sessions regularly thereafter once a month.

4. No Job Relations Trainer shall remain on the active list unless he puts on at least one 10-hour program in 90 days.

5. All Job Relations Trainers are expected to attend coaching sessions at the request of the T. W. I. District Office.

6. Job Relations sessions shall be limited to groups of 10 supervisors.

7. In order to be certified, participants must attend all 5 sessions in their logical sequence, participate satisfactorily, and present a problem.

8. For certification purposes, we will count the supervisor who brings an unsolved problem and, as it is being handled, decides he does not have all the facts, thereby shutting off further handling of the problem, because there is evidence that this person does understand the basic step of Job Relations. It is, of course, best to have him present the rest of the facts at a later session.

Job Relations Reference 2

TIPS FOR TRAINERS

Opening the Sessions

Have conference room ready and be there *ahead* of scheduled time—if you start on time, the group will make an extra effort to be prompt.

Urge some member of top management to introduce you to each group. Their appearance and endorsement of the program are important.

The 10-hour sessions of Job Relations are held so that supervisors will learn and practice the 4 steps and the application of the foundations. These sessions are not for the purpose of entertainment or morale building. Beware of "interesting" sessions.

Start at once and continue to emphasize that what we are doing is getting practice in the use of the method. In this practice we arrive at possible actions, but they are not to be construed as decisions. (We, in analyzing and applying the procedure, are not as close to the problem as the supervisor who actually must make the decision. We can definitely obtain experience in the use of the method by applying the method to another's problem. But, generally, any possible actions arrived at are not as reliable as those that are obtained through the use of the method by the supervisor who must actually make the decisions.)

Avoid a classroom atmosphere and above all do not be an expert. You are not running a one-man personnel relations bureau.

Don't take too much time to give your own experience and background. Your purpose is to set a pattern for the members to use in introducing themselves.

Stress on Method

Remember to follow and use the card. See that the members of the group follow and use the card in all discussions.

Constantly check yourself to see that you are not laying too much stress on something which particularly appeals to you at the expense of other points.

Show your enthusiasm for this program. Enthusiasm is contagious. After several groups, Job Relations may become an old story to you. Remember you are setting the standard for the group. The program can be no better than the trainer. Continue to be thorough at all times. A sloppy job by a trainer usually does more harm than good.

Bring out to the group the reasons for throwing the problems against the plan—to give them practice in using it. We are trying to acquire a skill. Your job during the ten hours is to sell the plan to all ten supervisors and give them basic training in its use.

Don't just read from the Manual—talk informally with feeling and expression. Make it live! Don't lecture or preach.

Working with the Group

Don't direct your remarks and questions to a favored few—get all members to participate.

Practice good relations with your groups. Don't argue—winning an argument may not convince the other fellow.

Don't try to imitate the personality of your Institute Conductor. Put your own personality into your performance, but stick to the ideas and thoughts outlined in the Manual.

Don't put yourself on a pedestal above the group. Be one of them. You will earn their respect if you do a good job putting on the sessions as outlined in the Manual.

Be alert when a member gives you an answer even when you are doing something else. Remember it and come back to him. Be constantly on the watch for contributions from individuals in the group. Allow them to express their views and don't try to rearrange or distort their contributions to suit some thought or idea you have in mind.

Be constantly on the lookout for background material contributed by the group with reference to the foundations. If necessary, ask members if they know of any instances where the foundations, if applied, would have prevented a problem from arising.

In an office group, particularly, supervisors should be told that they do not need to take notes and they should be specifically directed *not* to take notes on other supervisors' problems.

Handling Supervisors' Problems

Reference 3, the "Standard Procedure for Handling a Supervisor's Problem," is the final authority. (For the convenience of the trainer, a condensed form appears at the end of each session.) The steps in the procedure are to be followed *exactly*. They are designed to give the individual supervisor more practice. Be sure to get recognition of how the problem came up and the importance of preventive action. It is important to establish a real objective—see that the supervisor does not look just at the handling of the problem, but at the overall effect or results he wishes.

Avoid constant use of the *same* objectives *repeatedly* in all supervisors' problems. Vary them and make them appropriate to the problem. Help the supervisor reason out his objective but don't dominate his thinking.

Make "Fact" statements short and to the point.

Remember that all check-points in Step 2 are to be used. The objective, because it is used first, is no more important than the rest of the points.

When someone suggests a broad possible action like "get him interested" ask a "How" question, in order to bring the possible action down to something more specific. Otherwise, questions and answers are ambiguous when we test against possible actions.

If a supervisor claims he doesn't make decisions, point out that a recommendation is a decision. If a supervisor has a record of making good recommendations, then any that he makes are apt to be considered seriously by his superiors.

Don't let the group give you just any possible action. We want real thinking here. Use "What would you do based on these facts, if this problem were dumped into your lap?"

Be sure the members of the group understand that they are not being led to a decision. Decisions cannot be made in a conference room. We are never sure we have *all* the facts and we do not know the individuals concerned.

Again, the fact that nothing is done is often a decision. When a problem arises the supervisor sometimes decides not to take any action or that he should report the matter to his superiors. The fact that he decided to do nothing himself may be an important decision.

When a member of the group asks you a question pertinent to the supervisor's problem, refer it to the supervisor instead of trying to answer it yourself.

Don't indicate by your words or actions which possible action you think should be used. A trainer's function is to guide the thinking of the supervisor and the group through our various steps. We are not making a decision for the supervisor, but drilling on a method which each supervisor can use to arrive at his own decision on what action he should take. The supervisor should know the probable effect of any action on his objective, the individual, the group and production better than the trainer or any other member of the group.

Neither you nor the group is "solving" the supervisor's problem. We are developing our skill in using the foundations and the 4-step method. This is the tool that the supervisor can use to solve his own problems.

Don't expert (express personal opinions) by saying, "I think." Questions tempting you to do so should be redirected to the members of the group. A good trainer gets the group to do most of the thinking according to the pattern set by the Manual. Job Relations is designed to get *supervisors* to think and reason according to a pattern as a basis for sound actions, or as an aid to sound action.

Blackboard Work

Don't obstruct the view of the blackboard when discussing blackboard work.

Keep these three things in mind when at the board:

1. Write legibly.
2. Stand at the side of your work as much as possible.
3. Talk while writing.

Do not change supervisors' own words unless necessary to avoid highbrow phrasing. However, facts should be briefed on the board. Try whenever possible to get the sense and the meaning of the facts in from three to five words. Then check to make sure of meaning, but high-brow phrasing must be avoided. If someone gives AS A FACT "emotional instability" or "social maladjustment" make it specific. The facts—not their interpretation—are to be put on the board. Ask the supervisor to tell you what instances make him say that, and put on the board some specific thing like "had hysterics in office."

Make all blackboard work neat and readable. Talk or ask questions while at the blackboard in order to hold the group's attention.

Describing Practice

In the last 15 minutes of Session I spend some time enlarging on the procedure that will be followed in handling problems; explain that each supervisor will come to the head of the table and simply state the facts of the case. The trainer will place them on the board and the group will get experience in using the 4-step method. Emphasize that no comments or criticism will be made. It is important that the supervisors realize that they will not be criticized.

Emphasize at the end of Sessions II, III, and IV that to receive a certificate each supervisor must present a problem. Now that they know what the problems actually are, the regulations about certification mean something.

If people present problems which do not involve the direct relationship with someone supervised, the objective is apt to turn out to be of the "either or" or "whether or not" variety. The method applies in horizontal relationships, but for group practice we want to have a real objective to shoot at and therefore we want direct supervisory relationships.

If supervisors say they have no problems, and if they really are supervisors, ask them whether they have been doing some preventive work to keep problems from arising. This is particularly useful during Session IV when the trainer's problem has illustrated how a supervisor used both the foundations and the 4-step method to keep department conditions smooth and prevent problems from arising.

The Manual

A typographical code has been used to show whether material is:

- to be quoted
- to be presented in trainer's own words
- to be put on the board
- a direction to the Trainer

This code immediately precedes Session I (p. xxi).

Follow the suggested timing for each section. Experience has shown that the time indicated is needed to get the point over. If a particular section takes longer or shorter time than is indicated in the manual, then the timing gives you some idea as to how much you are ahead or behind. Start each session on time and close on time.

After each session you conduct, go over the manual and the problem handling to check yourself on omissions or failures to get a particular point over to the group. Keep studying your Manual, including the references. The Institute only gave you a start. Familiarity with the content of the Manual will improve your confidence and effectiveness as a trainer. If you are not sure of your interpretation of any section of the manual, check with the Job Relations men in the T. W. I. District Office.

Be very careful that any remarks you make supplementing the manual pertain to a particular paragraph in the manual. In other words, thoroughly analyze each paragraph or sentence, being sure you know what the meaning is. It is a common fault for trainers, in trying to supplement the manual, to be sidetracked and then have difficulty in getting back on the beam.

"Following the manual" does not mean sitting down and reading it. Learn it—then check yourself constantly. When there is board work to do, push your chair under the table and stay on your feet. Lean on the back of your chair to look at the manual but do not go back to your seat during the chart work in Sessions I and V, or during the blackboard work on a problem.

Follow your Manual. Omissions, overemphasis, or foreign material may lead you into trouble. Do not mark up the manual. Follow it exactly.

Job Relations Reference 3

STANDARD PROCEDURE FOR HANDLING A
SUPERVISOR'S PROBLEM

1. Ask supervisor to come to head of table and stay there until the problem handling is completed.

Ask supervisor—"Does this problem involve you and somebody who comes under your direction?"

> (Under no circumstances permit supervisor to use a hypothetical problem or one in which he was not involved as a supervisor.)

Say—"Have you taken action on your problem?"

> If the answer is "Yes," have him tell his problem up to, but not including, final action.

> To keep him from telling what the final action was, make a simple statement as to the reason for stopping. The purpose is to get better group participation—yet to give the supervisor the full benefit of his practice problem. Inform the supervisor that he is to tell the group about the incident or situation that made him realize he had a problem on which he had to take action, plus any fact-getting steps he then went through, but to stop before he gives any interpretation of the facts or mentions any decisions or actions.

> Under no circumstances, interrupt the man, even to keep him from telling the final action. If he generalizes, let him alone (unless the problem is very long) but when he finishes make some such remark as "you say this is always happening—let's take just one instance." In problems involving large numbers of people, try to reduce the problem to what involves only one person.

2. After he tells his problem, ask the supervisor in which one of the four ways this problem came to his attention (or comment on it, yourself).

> a. You sensed a change in your department.

> (EXAMPLE: Found changed relation or break in usual set-up.)

> b. You anticipated a change in your department.

> (EXAMPLE: You know a change is coming and want to prepare for it.)

> c. This one came to you.

> (EXAMPLE: An individual made a request or protested.)

d. You ran into this one.

(EXAMPLE: It just happened.)

The examples stated under a, b, c, d above are to be used only as necessary. Should the supervisor question what is meant, the purpose of bringing out how problems arise is to make supervisors more aware of the preventive work that may be done, particularly in regards to *a* and *b*.

STRESS *a* and *b* at every opportunity, pointing out that they are in the preventive areas. To vary this procedure after handling several supervisors' problems, you might ask any one of the group for the four ways that problems arise.

3. Ask supervisor: "Just what are *you* trying to accomplish?"

> (Do not erase this question when clearing the board at the conclusion of the first supervisor's problem. It will speed up your work if you do not have to rewrite it.)

The objective is something to shoot at. It may be difficult to determine. It may have to be changed in the course of handling the problem.

Help the supervisor to state his objective—but do not force him to accept someone else's statement. Question the objective if it seems short-sighted or mistaken.

Use of the following questions will be helpful:

What makes this a problem?

What do you want to have happen here?

What effect is this having on production?

Are any other people in the department concerned?

What results do you want to get out of this?

If the supervisor gives as his objective one that appears to be inadequate, such as "to discipline Joe," help him to get a long-range view by asking "why" in order to get him to see that the accomplishment he wants in the end is "to have Joe on the job regularly."

Get agreement from the group that the supervisor has chosen exactly what he is trying to accomplish. The following questions may be helpful:

Do you see exactly what he is aiming at?

Do you "get" the objective?

Would you have the same one?

What would you have in mind?

Do not write the objective given by the group on the board unless the supervisor is in agreement. The purpose of asking the other supervisors to participate is to get them thinking and give the supervisor telling the problem the benefit of their thoughts.

4. Ask supervisor for important facts and list them on the board as given by him. Do not number the facts. (Your board work should be brief but accurate. Write his statements in three or four words.)

Do not let this board work DRAG. Help the supervisor recall facts he has already mentioned. Putting down the facts is not a memory exercise. Suggest them. However, he is the referee—do not change or interpret his facts.

USE THE CARD FROM HERE ON OUT

Say—Let us look at our cards.

Make sure that everybody in the group is looking at his card before proceeding. Direct the questions to the supervisor.

> Ask—Have we reviewed the record and do we have those facts on the board? Do not let this go on a "yes" or "no" answer.
>
> Go through each sub-head in the same manner. Find out what facts were obtained by talking with the individual to get opinions and feelings. Show them on the board. Apply the "Tips for getting opinions and feelings" if appropriate. Ask why the worker did what he did.

This procedure may help get additional important facts and may preclude "talk with him" as a possible action in Step 2. Put additional facts, supplied in answer to the group's questions, on board. Do not separate them from the previously listed facts by a dotted line or space.

> Ask the supervisor: Are these all the facts needed for a decision?

If the supervisor who is presenting the problem says he does not have all the facts and if he has not yet taken action, the steps that will be taken to get more facts may be discussed. They will not be put on the board and there will be no discussion of possible actions or any other part of Step 2.

If the supervisor who is presenting the problem says he has already taken action, and during the discussion says that he did not have all the facts, handling of the problem continues.

> Ask the supervisor: Do you want the group to pitch in now?
>
> Ask group: Do you want to ask the supervisor any questions about this problem?
>
> Ask group: *If you were in the position of this supervisor, would you want any additional facts?*

If facts that seem trivial are suggested, you may want to ask the supervisor:

> Is that fact *important* in helping us to come to a decision in this problem?

By doing this, many times supervisors will wash out irrelevant facts. At this time you can, as part of the group, ask questions about the problem, but do not do this if group is working readily on these points.

All of the following information will probably not be needed in any one problem but the Trainer may need to ask the following "smoke-out questions" in the vein of, do you need to know —, would it make any difference if—?

Employee's job—just what he does

Time on present job and length of service with company

Work and training background before coming on with company

Present working environment

Work record: production, quality, housekeeping, absence, etc.

What (if any) recent changes have been made in the working conditions of the department which may affect the problem?

What is the working relationship between employee and foreman, from the employee's point of view?

Job rating of employee—how is he getting along?

Wage rate of employee—any recent change?

What (if any) company policies are involved?

Personal data concerning the employee

    a. Age
    b. Marital status and home life
    c. Outside activities: hobbies, social life, etc.

Personality, temperament, attitude of employee

What persons other than employees are involved?

What intermediate action (if any) has been taken in the problem? (This does not refer to a final solution.)

If a member of a group says, "But suppose it had been this way"—remind them that we deal only with facts. The Trainer must be particularly careful not to say "Let's assume" or "Suppose it had been."

Then ask — Are we reasonably sure we have the whole story?

If any member of the group says that he does not think there are enough facts, it is appropriate to ask him what part of the card brings him to that conclusion. The trainer may summarize by saying, "Then, if you were in the supervisor's shoes, you would feel you did not have the whole story and you would not be ready to decide on your action until you had more facts." This applies whether the supervisor presenting the problem has taken action or not.

5. Say—Let's take a look at the second step, Weigh and Decide. Write on board—
WEIGH AND DECIDE. Here is where we think about these facts.

> Quote the card —

>> The card says fit the facts together.

>> In fitting the facts together, let us see first if there are any contradictions; second, if there are any gaps that call for additional facts. *Discuss* these points.

>> Consider their bearing on each other. Do not make this either a statement or a "yes" or "no" question. This is part of the method.

> Do the facts indicate some possible actions?

> After this, again quote the card —

>> What possible actions are there? Write on board, under *Weigh and Decide*—Possible Actions.

> Explain that you are asking the group to suggest "Possible Actions" in order to:

>> get practice in Weighing and Deciding

>> show that there usually are several "Possible Actions"

> You are *not* trying to make the decision for the supervisor, or criticize what he has already done.

> Select one member of the group and ask: What would you do if you had this problem?

>> Ask him what facts he used. Do not let them be referred to as the "first and third"—name them. These are the facts which bear on each other and which produced the "possible action."

>> Ask the supervisor whether the action is possible within his company's policies and practices. If he says yes, write the "Possible Action" on the board.

Repeat with two more supervisors in the group.

A supervisor who points out in the discussion of Step 1 that he believes all the facts have not been obtained should not be asked for a possible action.

If anyone gives as a possible action such suggestions as "get the facts" or "find out why" it is handled by saying, "You mean you would want to get more facts before you decided on what you would do to handle this problem. Any supervisor must feel personally sure that he has the facts before he considers action—that is the meat of this Job Relations program. But at this point we will let the supervisors who feel there *are* enough facts, suggest the actions *they* would consider." When such a possible action as "Talk with the worker" is suggested, clarify the meaning. If it is "to find out," then it is not a possible action. If it is "to persuade him," re-phrase it before writing on the board. Get agreement to write it as "reason," "convince," or "persuade" and ask how he would do it to make it specific.

If additional facts are brought out at any time, write them on the board. After there are three or four "Possible Actions" on the board, check the first one by:

Asking the group whether this will accomplish the objective of:

Asking the supervisor about the objective, briefly—yes or no

Asking the supervisor about the probable effect on:

the individual
the group
production

Do not cross off Possible Actions even if the discussion proves them unwise. Crossing off may indicate to some the making of a decision by vote.

Remind the group that skill in Weighing and Deciding can be learned through practice. You become familiar with areas to explore, and what to be on the lookout for (but don't jump to conclusions).

If, in the discussion, there is some such statement made as "All these people coming from farms (or from stores, or all women, or any other generalization) are no good," or "All the fellows about to be called in the draft are hard to handle," the trainer must not let it stand. Point out that individuals are different, and that you can make a bad decision if you jump to conclusions about what they are like.

6. Have the supervisors state balance of his problem if action has been taken. Write it on the board. Make no comment on the action taken. Ask supervisor what facts he used in selecting this action. If action has not been taken, proceed to Steps 3 and 4. Your lead-in can be, "When you take action on this problem, are you going to handle this yourself, etc.—."

7. Check sub-heads under Step 3 with supervisor. Ask "Why" and "How" after sub-heads when pertinent. Get brief group discussion on timing the interval between reaching a decision and taking action. Ask group in every problem—"Let us look at our cards."

New supervisors are often concerned about being "by-passed." Remind them that they are by-passed when they fail to size up situations effectively in order to take the right action—the action that solves a problem.

Some supervisors feel they have no responsibility in connection with people whose work they are supervising because a staff department like employment, medical, or safety performs certain services, or because a superior handles complaints, grievances, or transfers, etc. But in all problems, the man closest to the individual employee does have a relationship with that person—he must make it good in order to get the most out of production. It will strengthen his leadership when he does. With new supervisors, particularly, there will be many requests for help on "What do I do when he says he won't do what I ask him to, or else shows that he doesn't want to?" Handle this in terms of the particular person involved. There aren't any general rules, and the supervisor has to stop looking for them. This is a real situation, and the only help anyone else can give him is to tell him to look at the whole situation—the persons involved, including himself, the effect on other people—try it and see how it works.

If a supervisor asks: "What do you think of what I did?" it will be helpful to say, "Well, let's take a look at what you were trying to accomplish. What were the results?"

Do not lose any chances to emphasize to the supervisors in your group that it is a definite part of the supervisor's job to realize just exactly how far his own responsibility and ability extend in the handling of Job Relations problems.

Remind supervisors to always ask themselves: "Is this something I should handle myself? Do I need help? Is this something I must pass on to my boss?"

Some cases will be brought in which involve people heading toward being fired. And sometimes that is the answer. Look at the effect on other people.

Is the effectiveness of the person more than the trouble he causes? In these days, we must keep everyone we can, if he is useful, but there are still some people who have to be fired.

8. Check sub-heads under Step 4 with supervisor. Use "when," "how often," and "what" after sub-heads when pertinent.

Ask how the supervisor can check results, and what he will look for.

9. Have the supervisor check whether or not objectives were accomplished or whether they may be accomplished if the problem has not reached final action. Let him tell "why."

10. Say, "Let's look at the other side of our card." (Make sure that they are looking at the cards.) Use the foundations in *preventive* sense. Ask supervisor, "Do any of our foundations for good relations apply in this problem?" "Could the use of any foundations have prevented this problem?"

Consider: "People must be treated as individuals."

If you are convinced that nothing on the foundation side applies, omit this step.

Thank the supervisor for contributing a problem. (Do not comment or pass judgment on actions or results.)

Job Relations Reference 4

A WAY OF LOOKING AT THE SUPERVISORY JOB

"Getting out the work" seldom runs along smoothly without interruption. About the time a group is working together smoothly, changes usually occur. Whether these changes are in the form of expanding schedules, improvements in methods, shifts in organization, or new employees, they always create problems. Supervisors need to know not only the operations and machines in their departments, but the people as well.

Expert knowledge of the job as an operator is not sufficient to make a good supervisor. In fact, such knowledge may make it difficult to notice the other supervisory problems. The supervisor needs to give attention to the particular characteristics of each individual for no two of them have exactly the same experience, abilities, and desires.

The supervisor will not always find it possible to apply these particular practices to his own situation, since they were used in different situations. But if he will look for the general ideas which the other fellows' practices illustrate, he will find that they can be applied to his problems too. These ideas have been derived from the experience of men in the shop.

It must be remembered that to the worker, a job means more than just a pay check every week or doing mechanical operations over and over between in-and-out whistles. It means that he is part of an organization, wherein he has a particular place. It means that he is a human being who wonders what kind of people his fellow-workers are, what they are going to expect of him, how he should approach his supervisor, etc. Consequently, job training is more than just teaching a shop skill. It includes helping the worker to adjust himself to his surroundings, giving him an idea of the organization of which he is a part, and the particular place he is to fill in it.

This is the point of view from which we approach these five sessions.

The supervisor facing hour by hour the difficulties of getting out the product may easily overlook the difficulties of his workers. It is natural for him to think most of results and to spend little time on people. Yet there are conditions in each department which hinder the employees from coming to full productiveness quickly and easily, and prevent the development of wholesome attitudes toward associates and the plant.

New supervisors can look back and remember a few things—what difficulties did you run into? Try to look at the department situation through the operator's eyes.

In getting out the product in the shop, the instructor or supervisor may fix his attention only upon materials. Look at the men—their minds, muscles, feelings, and attitudes. Observe them and talk with them. Notice what they do. Attempt to analyze their actions. Listen to their comments and encourage them to talk because the more clearly you know each operator as a person, the better you can supervise.

Understanding people is not a simple process. The supervisor or instructor who says, "I can size up a man as soon as I put him to work," is usually fooling himself. It will be helpful to notice some of the habits which actually hinder us in understanding them.

The "Die-Casting" Habit—Too often, as we observe individuals, we try to sort them into types or, to put it another way, to force them into imaginary molds which we have set up in our minds, much as the die-caster squirts metal into different kinds of molds. They may be different shapes before they go in, but they're all alike when they come out!

We feel that we have completely cataloged Bill Jones when we say that he is a "good mixer," that we have defined Tom Smith when we put him down as a "tough customer." But we can't do that with people, if we really wish to understand them. We must study each one from all sides, not pour them into molds or cast them into types.

The "Just Like" Habit—"He reminds me for all the world of Bill Brown," we say, and thereafter we notice most easily the traits which are like Bill Brown and ignore those which are different. Once we have made up our minds that he is "like Bill Brown," we close our minds to the possibility of his having other characteristics which we may need to know. We stop studying him, with the result that we never discover many of the interests and abilities which are part of him.

The "Go, No-Go" Habit—"I can tell whether a man will make a good operator in this job as soon as I see how he follows directions," said a supervisor. "If he listens carefully to my directions for doing the job and does it exactly as I tell him, he will make a good man. If he doesn't get the directions the first time, but tries to 'dope out' his own way of doing it, he seldom learns to do good work here." This supervisor, if he really does follow the way of thinking which he described, is classifying all employees into two classes: (1) Those who follow directions to the letter, and (2) those who try to figure out methods of their own. His gauge of men is two-valued, "go" or "no-go." There is no "in-between." He is applying an inspection technique, not an understanding one.

People are seldom "either-or." Studies of individuals show that approximately two-thirds of them have each of the commonly observed traits to a moderate degree. That is, they are close to the average in it, and that only a small percentage have markedly large or small degrees of any trait. Not "either-or" but "the degree to which" should be the guiding concept in studying people.

Similarly it is easy to fall into the habit of judging employees solely by how well they do that particular phase of the job in which the supervisor prides himself, over-looking their skill, or lack of skill, in other important parts of the work. For example, in one assembly and adjusting job, the supervisor had worked out a better way of tensioning a small spring. He took pride in this. It was very easy for him to fall into the habit of judging operators almost entirely by the way they tensioned this spring and to pass over other parts of the operation. People's reactions cannot be measured fairly with any single gauge. They are too complex.

The "Formula" Habit—Closely related to these "stereotype" ways of looking at people is the practice of dealing with each "type of person" in a certain set manner. It has been said that the way to "handle" the "oldtimer" is to "let him alone," that the best way to get along with the "chronic kicker" is to "lay down the law," that the way to teach the new worker is to "show him how" to do the job and "tell him what" the requirements are.

Of course, these methods work a good deal of the time with many of the people with whom supervisors and instructors have to deal. Otherwise they would not be so commonly accepted. But they become a hindrance when they are used as excuses for lumping people together in groups or types and avoiding the responsibility of trying to understand each person as an individual.

In short, people cannot be handled like piece parts or an apparatus. Each is an individual, different from every other. "Stereotyping" them, classifying them, standardizing them, or reducing them to formulas—habits of thinking that work well with inanimate things—often prove to be actual hindrances in handling people.

The "Standardization" Habit—Supervisors and instructors may become so accustomed to thinking in terms of standards that they look only for common responses of "the worker" and pay little attention to the special interests, abilities, and peculiarities of individual employees. Yet it is these special characteristics that yield fruitful contacts upon which to base effective supervision. It is the ways in which a person is different, and especially the ways in which he is superior to the "mine run" of people, which furnish the key to his special interests, for he tends to develop strong interests in the fields in which he possesses ability. The instructor has the problem of taking each of these unique and different personalities, finding out what he is like and to what he will respond, and fitting him into a job and into a working organization.

How to Understand the Individual Employee

How can the supervisor understand a person who comes into his organization well enough to fit him into the department? He can talk with him, question him, observe him, throw out conversational leads to draw him out, listen to him, and think and listen and think, seeking ever to look behind appearances and first impressions into the background of feelings, sentiments, and other reactions-to-experience which make up the man himself.

Keeping in mind that it is not a question of "either-or" but rather of "the degree to which," the supervisor can use the following questions in his study of each individual. In using each question, however, the supervisor must think constantly, "To what extent does he do this? In what degree is this true or not true of him? How far is this aspect important in this individual? Why does he react the way he does?" Here are the questions:

1. Is he "doing a good job?"

2. Does he fail to understand instructions?

3. Does his attention wander from the job?

4. Is he interested in his job?

5. How does he respond to recognition?

6. Does he stand on his own feet?

7. Does he seem ill-adapted to the job?

8. Does he get along well with the other people in the department?

Each of these questions may now be considered a little further.

1. *Is he doing a good job?*—Does he miss a part of the instructions when he is given a start on the new job? Most likely he does. Is he therefore stupid or careless? Not at all. He is merely human. The human mind has a perfect mechanism for avoiding overload. It simply ignores. If parts of the situation are wholly unrelated to the individual's past experience or to his present interest, he "pays no attention to them." If the total situation demanding his attention—for example, the new job—is complicated, his eyes and ears first grasp only those aspects which interest him most. If his experience with these is satisfying, he soon explores further and is ready for more instruction. The supervisor or instructor can help, first, by noticing the points of the job he seized upon at the beginning, as cues to his interests, and relating the rest of the instruction to these interests; and second, by noticing what points of the job the worker missed and bringing these to his attention as soon as he is ready for them. Are you sure that he knows just what you expect of him? Have you over-sold the job and is he let down?

2. *Does he fail to understand instructions?*—Does he misinterpret them? Does he fail to catch the point of the explanation? Does he seem "a bit thick?" The easy way out is to label such a person "dumb" and thus avoid all responsibility for making an efficient operator of him. This, however, neither saves the man nor gets the work done, and what is more it is usually unnecessary. Most workers who have passed the employment office are high enough in mental capacity to learn readily the jobs to which they have been assigned. When they fail to understand, it is not from "dumbness" but from *narrowness of experience*. They are like the city boy who, on his first visit to a farm, tried to get a pail of water by calmly holding up the pump handle, waiting for the water to come. Why shouldn't he? He had seen hydrants with pull-up handles but he had never seen a pump in a well.

The worker who learns slowly because of narrow experience can usually be trained by patient, well-planned instruction and often makes a superior operator. Cues to his background and his interests may be gained by encouraging him to talk about the job, listening to him without interruptions, and giving attention as much to what he takes for granted as to what he actually says. Gaps in his background can be filled by giving him actual experience in the shop.

The worker who misinterprets instructions, and thus makes mistakes, is a similar problem. On account of the narrowness of his experience he fails to understand. Where others might have got meaning, he draws a blank because he doesn't know the "code." Yet he fears to reveal his ignorance. What does he do? He bridges the gap by using his imagination and, whenever he guesses wrong, he makes mistakes. The remedy is to make connection with his meager experience by finding out as much about it as possible and to win his confidence to the point where he is willing to ask questions. It often helps to have him repeat instructions in his own words: "Now just to be sure I've made it clear, tell me what it is you're going to do."

Care in explaining shop terms will help greatly. One worker tells of his first day in the shop thus: "The boss gave me a big pan of little gadgets and said, 'Take these piece parts over to that bench and "mike" 'em. The "max." and "min." are six and ten.' Then off he went and I spent the next 3 hours trying to figure out what mike, min., and max. had to do with the job, and what I was supposed to do with the pan of gadgets."

Ignorance of shop terms and shop customs is by no means confined to "new" employees fresh from the employment office. Picture an experienced employee newly transferred from a distant department, trying to adjust himself to a new location and learn a wholly new kind of job. During his years on the old job he has gone along, paying little attention to other organizations, yet now on the new job he is ashamed to reveal his ignorance. He is grateful to the instructor who will take the trouble to discover the limits of his experience and give him the help he needs.

3. *Does his attention wander from the job?*—Does he seem to be oversensitive to noises, changes in light and ventilation, presence of other workers or passers-by? If so, he is merely responding naturally—acting "like a human being." Most individuals find it hard *not* to pay attention to all that is going on around them, especially to noises and people.

The new worker, in addition to mastering his skill, has to become accustomed to a "total situation" which is strange and fascinating. In fact, a part of any skill is an ability to ignore everything except the activity itself—to concentrate one's attention on it. Witness the ability of the champion athlete to forget his gallery and lose himself in the game.

Complete absorption in a task and disregard of surroundings amid the distracting noise and activity of a manufacturing plant is not a natural act. It is an achievement—that is, it can be learned. Fortunately, most workers are able to learn it for themselves in a relatively short time. Sometimes it is possible to help the worker who is unusually sensitive to distraction by placing him in a less exposed location where noises are either more uniform or monotonous, or by transferring him to work which requires a broader spread of attention or which includes dealing with a large number of people.

4. *Is he interested in his job?*—Does he fail to put forth the effort necessary to learn to do the job well? A man will have an interest in a job if he feels that it is in harmony with his own purposes, that it is "getting him somewhere." If he can identify the job with himself, see its connection with his own life, with his cherished ambition, then he is "interested in the job" in the same sense that a man who buys an interest in a business is "interested in" that business. When this happens there is no trouble about effort.

But often the new worker cannot see any relation between his own plan for the future and the job to which he is assigned. The instructor can explain to the worker how upgrading takes place and what avenues of advancement are open to him if he is efficient in each job along the line. Some young workers are victims of the "white-collar" craze; their only idea of advancement is to get out of the shop and into the office, without any clear understanding of the possibilities of either. A supervisor or instructor can often render a real service to such young people by giving them facts regarding the values of shop experience, no matter where later promotions or transfers may lead, and helping them to think over their plans and ambitions in the light of these facts rather than on the basis of family or personal prejudice regarding "overalls" or the "white collar."

Occasionally the supervisor or instructor finds an individual who has "hitched his wagon to a star" far beyond the limits of his capacity, background, and education. He may have to help such a person to get his feet on the ground. On the other hand, some learners in the shop seem to have no definite ambition or plan of action for their lives at all. By talking with them and becoming better acquainted, the instructor may be able to discover such an ambition and help the worker to connect his job with it.

Under war conditions it is a powerful stimulus to show each man what he and the department do for the war effort.

One instructor, in training a man to turn out a bushing on a turret lathe, said, "This part will be hardened and ground and put into a molding machine to guide the mold down into place accurately each time it is closed to mold a casting."

Many instructors make it a point to tell the operator how his product will be used: "This goes into an airplane to show the pilot so and so—." "This goes into an instrument panel to show so and so—."

In a highly specialized factory it is difficult to provide the interest which the old craftsman felt in the product of his hands because it was all his own, from raw material to finished master piece. The modern shop, where the worker can see the whole product fabricated before his eyes, provides an opportunity to revive this kind of interest. For the same reason, moving workers about from job to job until they have become familiar with all the operations on a particular product adds to their interest. Each job takes on meaning and significance as its relation to other operations and to the whole product is seen. The worker can "see what he is doing" and see that it is worthwhile.

Likewise, a worker has more interest in his machine if he understands how it works, the principles of its operation, what it can do, and just as important, what it cannot do; i.e., the limits of its operation. When the worker knows these things, instead of blindly following the directions of the machine setter or the equipment man, he takes an interest in the machine. Because he feels that he understands it, he comes to identify it with himself, just as he does the job in which he "has an interest." It becomes his machine, and thus a new interest in the job is born.

A more simple key to the worker's interest is some activity which he enjoys doing for its own sake. One supervisor makes a practice of talking with the new worker about his hobbies. He discovers what the worker likes to do and often is able to relate the job to these interests, or to help him transfer to a job he enjoys.

Knowledge of his own progress stimulates the learner's interest. Supervisors long ago discovered the value of operators' performance records as an incentive, especially when presented in graphic form. We like to beat our own record, to see ourselves grow in skill, and most of us like to engage in rivalry with others. Rivalry of output, however, is a form of stimulation which has to be handled wisely, especially during the training period. Progress in learning does not always register in daily output. While learning correctness of "form" and developing the ability to reach quality standards, output may not show a daily increase and the worker should not judge his progress by it. The instructor can prevent discouragement and loss of interest by directing his attention to this fact.

Then there is the matter of social approval. Any experienced supervisor knows the value of recognition as a stimulation of interest in the job. Praise is discussed further in a different connection below.

The effectiveness of all these ways of reaching the worker's interests and relating them to the job lies in the fact that a man reacts as a whole. We sometimes talk of training his muscles or his brain or his hands. We can't. His whole self is being trained by every experience he has. We teach the man, not his hand. When he has mastered a skill, the whole man has it, uses it, and is proud of it. The man himself has ambitions to which the job may or may not be related. The man himself enjoys doing it, or is indifferent to it. The man himself basks in the appreciation of his fellows when they recognize that he has done the job well. Anything which connects with his interests affects all parts of him. His eye brightens, his mind becomes more alert, his hand more sure. Recognition of success in one part of the job reacts to heighten his interest in the job as a whole, and he does the whole job better. Conversely, failure in any part of the job depresses the whole man, his work and his attitude toward the job—unless he and his supervisor regard the failure as a challenge, analyze it, and learn how to overcome it.

The largest factor with which a supervisor or instructor has to deal is his worker's "interests." This emphasizes again the need for the supervisor to become well acquainted with his workers as persons, to understand their backgrounds of experience, their hopes and purposes for the future, their bents and special abilities, all in order that he may help them to discover real and lasting connections between themselves and their jobs.

5. *How does he respond to recognition?*—Does praise stimulate him? How does he take criticism?

Experienced supervisors know that a little recognition adds zest to the job and stimulates a man's efforts. This is especially true of the learner, because he feels insecure and uncertain about himself anyhow. Building his confidence is part of the job.

Recognition of good work can be given in many ways. Posting records of progress has been discussed above. Advancement to a harder or more important job stimulates a learner just as it does an experienced worker. Whenever he is ready for a more difficult step in the learning of the job, the instructor can use this for stimulation by saying, "You've done well with that. You're ready for this harder job now."

The most tangible form of recognition is, of course, the weekly pay envelope. An increase in his rate is a visible goal. But so many factors over which the supervisor has no control enter into determination of wages that he finds other forms of recognition also necessary as instruction incentives. Using an advanced learner occasionally as an instructor is a form of recognition. It adds prestige and gives a bit of recognition to those who are competent.

Praise in the presence of the group is an effective form of recognition, so long as it is fair. It is usually stronger than praise in private but more difficult to give because the members of the group are always making comparisons. Both approval and correction are necessary, but criticism given before the group usually results in confusion or resentment.

The new worker learns more from praise than from censure. The reason is simple. He is blundering about, seeking the right way to do each part of the job. When he happens upon a right way, and the instructor approves it, he knows he has got that part of the job, and seeks to repeat it. At the same time he experiences a glow of satisfaction which spurs him on to master other parts of the job. But suppose he tries a wrong way and is "bawled out?" What has he learned? Simply that one way is wrong. He still does not know a right way and may try many other wrong ones before he finds a right one. Meanwhile he feels discouraged because of the disapproval. The alert supervisor will of course seize such a moment to demonstrate again the "right way" to do the operation, though that is beside the point here. It is often necessary to point out mistakes but, even at its best, censure or adverse criticism helps the learner too slowly on his way to skill. Instead it is better to catch him as often as possible doing the right thing, even by chance, and speed him on his way with a word of appreciation.

6. *Does he stand on his own feet?*—Does he lean on the supervisor too much, or go to the opposite extreme and act as if he knows it all?

Most new workers are a bit fearful and lacking in confidence, some more and some less. They show it in curious and contradictory ways, as the above questions suggest. A little fear when facing a new situation serves to awaken most persons to greater alertness and effort. They are able to rise to the occasion and soon overcome their fears. They "take things in their stride." Yet there are many individuals who lack emotional balance, who have not learned to take life as it comes, to face reality as adults. It is important, however to remember the caution about "die-casting" people into molds, to notice "the degree to which" the individual lacks emotional balance. Differences in individuals range all the way from the person who adjusts himself to the job situation promptly, stands on his own feet and quietly tackles everything in a matter-of-fact way, to the person who leans on others and expects favors, who covers his fears with over boldness, or who seeks to "make a good impression" instead of concentrating his attention on learning the job.

While the supervisor or instructor cannot go along indefinitely trying to help a maladjusted person "grow up," he can often add to the timid man's confidence by pointing out his successes and, on the other hand, bring a bluffer back to reality by facing him with the demands of the job. He is interested at all times in each operator's reactions to the job and to his fellow-workers, because they are facts which affect his doing the job, his attitude toward it, and toward the whole organization.

7. *Does he seem ill-adapted to the job?*—In spite of the best efforts of line supervisors and personnel organization, employees are sometimes placed on jobs they cannot do satisfactorily. Two cautions are in order here, however.

First: Do not assume that an employee is a misfit in a job until he has been fully and correctly instructed on that job and has shown that he cannot do it successfully. Many men have been called misfits on jobs they never had a fair chance to learn. Often a slow learner makes an excellent operator. It is a misfortune for him if he has to begin the job under a supervisor or instructor without the patience and willingness to instruct.

Second: Do not assume that when a worker is a misfit in one job he is useless. Any supervisor of long experience could tell stories of "misfits" who found other places where they made good. Few misfits are totally unfit.

Get acquainted with the employee, win his confidence, discover what he can do and likes to do, find out his difficulties on the job, and see that he either learns it or gets a fair trial at other jobs for which he is better adapted.

8. *Does he get along well with other people in the department?*—Sometimes men know how to do their jobs well, and yet they are not effective because they do not get along well with the people with whom they work.

Consider whether any differences in your relationships with the various people are part of the situation.

You may need to re-align the team in order to get a group to work together.

SUMMARY

Good supervision is not a skill which can be mastered over night—human beings are complex. But it is a skill in which you improve on the job, and one which gives returns to you, your department, your plant, and the war effort.

A Supervisor Gets Results Through People

FOUNDATIONS FOR GOOD RELATIONS

1. Let Each Employee Know How He Is Getting Along

Figure out and tell him what you expect.
Point out ways to improve.

2. Give Credit When Due

Recognize extra or unusal performance.
Tell him while it's fresh.

3. Tell An Employee in Advance About Changes That Will Affect Him

Tell him WHY if possible.
Get him to accept the change.

4. Make Best Use of Each Person's Ability

Look for ability not now being used.
Never stand in an employee's way.

People Must Be Treated As Individuals

JOB RELATIONS TRAINING
U.S. Civil Service Commission

HOW TO HANDLE A PROBLEM

DETERMINE OBJECTIVES

Step 1 — Get the Facts
Review the record.
What policies, rules, regulations apply?
Talk with individuals concerned and get opinions and feelings.
Be sure you have the whole story.

Step 2 — Weigh and Decide
Fit the facts together and consider their
    bearing on each other.
What possible actions are there?
Check each action against objectives
    weighing effect on individual, group, and
    production.
Select the best actions.

Step 3 — Take Action
Should I handle this?
Who can help in handling?
Should I refer this to my supervisor?
Consider proper time and place.
Explain and get acceptance.
Don't pass the buck.

Step 4 — Check Results
How soon and how often will I check?
Watch for changes in output, attitude, and
relationships.
Did my action help production?
  WERE OBJECTIVES ACCOMPLISHED?

Publications from Enna

From Enna's new classics by Shigeo Shingo to our books and training packages regarding operational excellence, Enna provides companies with the foundation of knowledge and practical implementation ideas that will ensure your efforts to internalize process improvement. Reach your vision and mission with the expertise within these world-class texts. Call toll-free (866) 249-7348, visit us on the web at www.enna.com to order, or request our free product catalog.

Enjoy the rest of the books in our T.W.I. Training Series:

Job Instruction: Sessions Outline and Materials

Job Instruction, a short, intensive training program, was developed in order to provide skills in leadership to new and experienced supervisors alike. Contained within the Job Instruction book are samples, scenarios, and discussion topics which give you the tools necessary to properly instruct new workers and do away with waste and accidents, as well as cut down the time it takes to get a new worker 'up to speed' on his job.
ISBN 978-1-897363-92-8 | 2009 | $34.99 | Item: **922**

Job Methods: Sessions Outline and Materials

In teaching you the method behind the job and how to properly break down a job into its most fundamental parts, this book aims to teach you how to reduce wasteful behavior and wasteful steps within a job. The training material within provides you with worksheets, forms and sample scenarios to give you practice in scrutinizing and simplifying jobs.
ISBN 978-1-897363-93-5 | 2009 | $34.99 | Item: **923**

Job Relations: Sessions Outline and Materials

Job Relations was developed in order to provide management with a tool whereby supervisors could acquire skills in leadership. Contained within the Job Relations book are sample scenarios, discussion topics and instructional diagrams that relate the supervisor and his subordinates, show the dynamic of such a relationship and provide a way of looking at and dealing with these relationships that will benefit everyone in the company.
ISBN 978-1-897363-94-2 | 2009 | $34.99 | Item: **924**

Union Job Relations: Sessions Outline and Materials

Union Job Relations was developed concurrently with Job Relations in order to provide stewards with a way to acquire skills in leadership within their company and union. Contained within the Union Job Relations book are sample scenarios, discussion topics and instructional diagrams that relate the steward to his union, supervisors and the union members he is responsible for, shows the dynamic of such relationships and provide a way of looking at and dealing with these relationships that will benefit everyone in the company.
ISBN 978-1-897363-95-9 | 2009 | $34.99 | Item: **925**

To Order: Enna Corp., 1602 Carolina Street, Unit B3, Bellingham, WA 98229

Program Development Institute

The Program Development Institute was established in order to train people in setting up and implementing an entire training program within their company. Enclosed are worksheets, examples and practice problems to assist in developing the program as a training coordinator. With this book you will learn how to step back and look at the company as a whole, before implementing training and improvements.
ISBN 978-1-897363-96-6 | 2009 | $34.99 | Item: **926**

Problem Solving Training: Sessions Outline and Materials

The Problem Solving workbook instructs on how to properly Isolate, Breakdown, Question and Solve problems. From detailing just how you know you have a problem to charts and diagrams that will assist you in solving the problem, this book is a must read for anyone who deals with production on a daily basis.
ISBN 978-1-926537-00-9 | 2009 | $34.99 | Item: **927**

Bulletin Series

Based on the simple premise that in order to function there has to be an organized structure that recognizes that ongoing training is an investment that will always pay for itself the T.W.I. Bulletin Series is packed with ideas, concepts, and methods that will produce results. Contained within are bulletins that will assist in selecting supervisors, strengthening management and achieving continuous results.
ISBN 978-1-897363-91-1 | 2008 | $34.99 | Item: **914**

Other Books by Enna

Mistaken Kanbans

Let Mistaken Kanbans be your roadmap to guide you through the steps necessary to implement and successful Kanban System. This book will help you to not only understand the complexities of a Kanban System but gives you the tools necessary, and the guidance through real-life lessons learned, to avoid disastrous consequences related to the improper use of such systems.
ISBN 978-1-926537-10-8 | 2009 | $27.99 | Item: **919**

The Toyota Mindset

From the brilliant mind of a legend in the LEAN manufacturing world comes the reasoning behind the importance of using your intellect, challenging your workers and why continuous improvement is so important. For anyone who wishes to gain insight into how the Toyota Production System came to be or wants to know more about the person behind TPS this book is a must read!
ISBN 978-1-926537-11-5 | 2009 | $34.99 | Item: **920**

The Toyota Way in Sales and Marketing

Many companies today are trying to implement the ideas and principles of Lean into non-traditional environments, such as service centers, sales organizations and transactional environments. In this book Mr. Ishizaka provides insight on how to apply Lean operational principles and Kaizen to these dynamic and complicated environments.

ISBN 978-1-926537-08-5 | 2009 | $28.99 | Item: **918**

Training Packages

5S Training Package

Our 5S Solution Packages will help your company create a sustainable 5S program that will turn your shop floor around and put you ahead of the competition. All of the benefits that come from Lean Manufacturing are built upon a strong foundation of 5S. Enna's solution packages will show you how to implement and sustain an environment of continuous improvement.

Version 1: Sort, Straighten, Sweep, Standardize and Sustain
ISBN 978-0-973750-90-4 | 2005 | $429.99 | Item: **12**
Version 2: Sort, Set In Order, Shine, Standardize and Sustain
ISBN 978-1-897363-25-6 | 2006 | $429.99 | Item: **17**

Study Mission to Japan

We are excited to present an exclusive trip to the birthplace of Lean. We provide a one-week unique tour at a reasonable all-inclusive price that will guide you to a better understanding of Lean Manufacturing principles. Enna has exclusive access to Toyota and Toyota suppliers due to our publications of Dr. Shigeo Shingo's classic manuscripts. You will have one-on-one access to Japanese Lean Executives and learn from their experiences and solutions. We also offer custom private tours for executive management teams over 12 people. Join us on our next tour by visiting www.enna.com/japantrip and register on-line or by telephone at: +1 (360) 306-5369

To Order:

Mail orders and checks to:
Enna Products Corporation
ATTN: Order Processing
1602 Carolina Street, Unit B3
Bellingham, WA 98229, USA
Phone: +1 (360) 306-5369　•　Fax: (905) 481-0756
Email: info@enna.com

We accept checks and all major credit cards.
Notice: All prices are in US Dollars and are subject to change without notice.

To Order: Enna Corp., 1602 Carolina Street, Unit B3, Bellingham, WA 98229

Printed in the United States
by Baker & Taylor Publisher Services